TELEPHONE
FUND RAISING

Nonprofit Management and Finance
Series Editor: VIRGINIA WHITE

A Continuation Order Plan is available for this series. A continuation order will bring delivery of each new volume immediately upon publication. Volumes are billed only upon actual shipment. For further information please contact the publisher.

TELEPHONE FUND RAISING

Jonathan A. Segal • Janet B. Allen

PLENUM PRESS • NEW YORK AND LONDON

Library of Congress Cataloging in Publication Data

Segal, Jonathan A.
  Telephone fund raising.

Allen County Public Library
Ft. Wayne, Indiana

(Nonprofit management and finance)
Includes bibliographical references and index.
1. Telephone fund raising—United States. I. Allen, Janet B. II. Title. III. Series.
HV41.9.U5S44   1986   361.7'068'1   86-20534
ISBN 0-306-42340-5

© 1987 Plenum Press, New York
A Division of Plenum Publishing Corporation
233 Spring Street, New York, N.Y. 10013

Printed in the United States of America

To my parents

J.A.S.

For my father, John L. Allen

J.B.A.

PREFACE

There was a time when bake sales, raffles, and the like provided non-profit-making organizations with the funds they needed to flourish. Those days have long passed. Non-profit-making organizations now find themselves competing with one another for public and private support just to survive.

The organizations that will survive are the ones that are not afraid of sophisticated fund-raising methods. Telephone fund raising is such a method. There is virtually no limit to the amount of money telephone fund raising can bring your organization. Telephone fund raising is so successful because it is personal. It allows for dialogue. More specifically, it allows the caller to answer questions, deal with complaints, negotiate hard, and stress those aspects of the program that interest the potential contributor most. No method of fund raising other than a personal visit can do this. And, of course, visiting all your potential contributors personally would be impossible.

This book provides you with all the information you need to develop and maintain a lucrative telephone fund-raising program on your own. The general principles of telephone fund raising apply universally. Therefore, the principles will work for you, whatever your cause. They also will apply whatever your need. Whether you need a long-term telephone fund-raising program bringing in money at a steadily increasing rate over the years or a short-term program lasting one month, one week, or even one day, this book is for you.

There are a few rules particular to political groups, however. These special rules have been incorporated throughout the book. There also are a few rules particular to organizations that wish to have a one-time, short-term program (which we refer to as a one-shot deal). These special rules have also been incorporated throughout the book.

This book describes a model telephone fund-raising program; a per-

vii

fect program, in fact. We tell you what a perfect caller would do in almost every situation. We tell you how to find only the best callers. We tell you how to conduct a flawless training session. We tell you how the ideal pledge collection system works.

We realize your world will not be perfect. We know that sometimes you will have to deviate from the ideal. That is why we have taken pains to provide you not only with the rules but also with the rationale behind them. When you need to deviate from the ideal, keep in mind the rationale behind the rule. Try to fulfill the spirit of the rule, at least. This will insure that you come as close as possible to the ideal.

Chapter 1 discusses the actual phone call, emphasizing the negotiating process in particular. Chapter 2 discusses everything you need to know about callers: how to find them, choose them, train them, pay them, and so on. Chapter 3 discusses the mechanics of calling: who to call, how to prepare for the call, where to call from, when to call, and so on. And, finally, Chapter 4 discusses how to structure and administer a telephone fund-raising program, large or small.

Although we discuss planning and setting up your program at the end of the book, it actually will be the first thing you will do. We put these sections at the end of the book because to understand how to plan and administer your telephone fund-raising program effectively, you need to know all that telephone fund raising entails. But this does not mean that you should not be mindful of planning and administration as you go through the book. Keep in mind these two questions especially:

1. How much money you need to raise.
2. How much start-up money you have.

Of course, the book will show you how to arrive at the answers to these key questions.

The Authors

CONTENTS

1

NEGOTIATING LARGE PLEDGES

Asking High

Everyone you call can give $50. After all, that is not even $1 a week. It is not even 15¢ a day. Of course, your program is worth 15¢ a day, so expect at least $50 from everyone you call.

If you expect $50, you must ask for significantly more. How much more? Use the rule of five. If you expect $50, start each call with a $250 request. Likewise, if you expect $100, begin each call with a $500 request.

Why ask so high? First of all, if you do not ask for big pledges, you will not get big pledges. But that is not the only reason. Starting with a high request immediately alerts potential contributors that you expect something substantial from them. And it gives you a great deal of negotiating room, which is the key to getting big pledges.

Negotiating is a game. You make a move, they make a move, and so on. By asking high, you get more moves. Never make the mistake of asking immediately for what you expect. That severely limits your number of moves. Consequently, it limits the amount of money you will get. So start each call with a high request.

If the person commits at the top level, well and good. If you hear a laugh or negative response from the other end of the line, move quickly to the next level. There is no need to linger at the top level. Save your intense negotiations for the following levels.

Your second request should be considerably lower than your first— about half. If your first request is $500, your second request should be about $250. Telephone fund raising is a friendly tug-of-war. By giving up a lot of rope early—by dropping to $250—you let potential contributors know that you are willing to compromise and that you expect them to do the same.

1

If the person says no to the $250 request, hold on to the rope. You have given up half, showing your willingness to compromise. Now you must give up only a few inches at a time. Your next requests should drop in $50 increments. Ask for $200, then $150 followed by $100 and $50.

Although you anticipate pledges of $50 and up, this does not mean that you should not pursue pledges below $50. By asking for $500, you will be getting $300, $200, and $100 pledges. These big pledges will make up for the little pledges. So if the potential contributor says no to $50, ask for $35, then $25, and finally $10. You might as well get something. You have already invested your time, energy, and money. Besides, it is not unusual for a $10 supporter one year to give $250 the next year. In sum, here is a logical progression to follow: $500, $250, $150, $100, $50, $35, $25, and, finally, $10.

Now that you understand the need for asking high and gradually working your way down, the next step is creating a dialogue. Three sample negotiations follow. They show how a good caller progresses toward a pledge. Things to notice: the friendly style, the way the caller guides the conversation toward the pledge, and the way the caller integrates specific pledge requests with information about the program and its needs. Afterward, we will analyze in detail the components of the negotiations.

The three dialogues that follow have neither a beginning nor an ending. What you will be reading is the heart of the negotiation process. Of course, all of your calls will have a beginning and an ending. But because the middle—the negotiation process—is the most difficult to master, we address it first. We discuss the beginning and the ending later.

In Dialogue 1, the call is made on behalf of an art museum; in Dialogue 2, on behalf of a political action group; and in Dialogue 3, on behalf of a community group. Regardless of the nature of your group, read all three dialogues. The negotiating skills they illustrate apply universally.

Sample Dialogues

Dialogue 1 (Art Museum)

CALLER: So, can I put you down for a $500 pledge?

POTENTIAL CONTRIBUTOR: You're talking to the wrong person for that kind of money.

CALLER: Let's try something more moderate, a gift of $250. You can break this pledge into two installments of $125. That means you will pay $125

now and $125 six months from now. That will make you a member of
the Creative Circle. As a member of the Creative Circle you'll receive
invitations to advance private showings of exhibits and to all our other
special events. In addition, you will receive a pass entitling you and the
other members of your family to free admission. And, of course, this gift
will be tax-deductible. How about it, Mr. Conrad? For less than $1 per
day, you can become a member of the Creative Circle.

POTENTIAL CONTRIBUTOR: You're still way out of my league. Look, I have
a family of five to support. And one of my kids is in college. I don't have
to tell you what that costs. So not this year.

CALLER: I can appreciate your situation, Mr. Conrad. Many people I have
spoken with this evening are in similar situations. What they found
manageable is a more moderate pledge of $150. You have a family of
five. Well, this pledge is less than 60¢ a week per family member. I think
the Art Museum is worth that, and I hope you do, too. You know, Mr.
Conrad, I want to make this as comfortable for you as possible, so I'll
break this pledge into four quarterly installments of $37.50. That means
that all you need to give now is $37.50. Can I put you down for a tax-
deductible pledge of $150?

POTENTIAL CONTRIBUTOR: I'll have to think about it and talk it over with
my wife. Call me back next week.

CALLER: Well, if at all possible, I would like to arrive at some commitment this evening. As you may know, we have been severely hurt by
recent budget cuts. We are currently negotiating for matching funds
from the government. We need your commitment to get theirs. The
amount of money we get from them depends on the amount of money
we get from people like you. That's why I would like to put you down
for a pledge this evening. How about a $100 pledge? If you decide to
give more, well, naturally, that would be great. But, for now, at least we
can count on you for $100. I'll even break it into two semiannual install-
ments of $50 to make it easier for you. By the way, Mr. Conrad, this
pledge is only about 30¢ a day, less than the cost of a cup of coffee. Of
course, the Art Museum is worth a cup of coffee a day. So can I put you
down for a pledge of $100? This pledge will make you a member of the
Friends' Circle. This is our most popular club. As a member, you'll
receive all sorts of benefits including announcements of museum exhibits and special events, a card entitling you and your family to a 30%
discount on admission, and much more.

POTENTIAL CONTRIBUTOR: I don't know. How did you get my name,
anyway?

CALLER: Quite frankly, you are living in an area that is supportive of us.
As a matter of fact, you could be the third person this evening in Spring-
field to join the Friends' Circle. Please, Mr. Conrad, we're counting on
you. Can I put you down for a $100 pledge? The dollars you contribute
will go directly into the fund for the purchase of new paintings. And,
once again, your contribution will be tax-deductible.

POTENTIAL CONTRIBUTOR: All right.

CALLER: Great! I have one more request. I would like to put this on your credit card. This will save us time and money. The money we save will mean more money allocated to art rather than to administrative costs. Can I put this on your credit card?

POTENTIAL CONTRIBUTOR: No problem.

Dialogue 2 (Political Action Group)

CALLER: Can I put you down for a $500 pledge?

POTENTIAL CONTRIBUTOR: No way, I don't have that kind of money. Besides, I'm not going to give a penny to your organization, even though I do believe in your lobbying efforts. That new lobbyist you hired, Charles Lind, rubbed me the wrong way.

CALLER: I can understand your being angry that we hired Charles Lind. It was a mistake on our part, and we publicly apologized. I hope you realize that he no longer works for us and that we intend to be more selective in future hiring. Please accept my apologies on behalf of the organization. While we did make a mistake in hiring Charles Lind, we have made wonderful progress in other areas. For example, last year we were able to defeat three bills that would have wiped out our political gains of the last decade. We succeeded in protecting your interests. That's why I'm hoping you can help us with a $300 gift. You can pay this in quarterly installments of $75 each. This gift actually is less than $1 a day. We think sensible political action is worth $1 a day and hope you do, too. How about it? Are you agreeable to a $300 pledge?

POTENTIAL CONTRIBUTOR: No way. Since you took the time to call and explain your situation, I'll send $35 to help your lobbyists. But that is it.

CALLER: Thank you very much for your offer of $35. But this year we need a little more. As you probably know, our interests are not being represented at the national level. I am hoping that you can give us that $35 now and again three more times throughout the year. That would be a total pledge of $140 paid in quarterly installments. And that's not even $3 a week. As a matter of fact, that's less than 50¢ a day. How about it, Ms. Ford?

POTENTIAL CONTRIBUTOR: Don't you listen? I said $35. Now you say $140!

CALLER: I don't mean to pressure you, and I have been listening to what you are saying. I just thought that you might give us the $35 four times this year to boost our lobbying efforts. I have an idea. Let's compromise. Why don't you give us $35 now and then an additional $35 in six months? That would be a total pledge of $70. Is that all right?

POTENTIAL CONTRIBUTOR: I'm not going to commit a penny six months in advance.

CALLER: Okay, how about this? Can you give us $50 all at once? That's only an extra 30¢ a week beyond your original offer. How about that,

Ms. Ford? One dollar a week to insure that Congress responds to our strong constituency.

POTENTIAL CONTRIBUTOR: Okay.

Dialogue 3 (Community Group)

CALLER: Can I put you down for a pledge of $250?

POTENTIAL CONTRIBUTOR: I'm sorry, I'm a senior citizen. I don't have that kind of money.

CALLER: I understand. Let's try something more moderate, a gift of $150. You can pay this in three consecutive monthly installments of $50. And you know, Mr. Peters, this pledge is less than $3 a week. As our way of saying thank-you, we'll send you a Community Center travel bag. I have one, and it's terrific! By the way, this contribution also will be tax-deductible.

POTENTIAL CONTRIBUTOR: It sounds like you're asking me for an awful lot.

CALLER: We're asking you to make the Community Center one of your top giving priorities this year. Without strong public support, we might have to close the Center. We're fighting for our survival. I'm confident that we can survive. But I'm realistic and know that we can't without public support. This truly is our make-or-break year, and I hope you will help us make it with a pledge of $150 to be paid in consecutive monthly installments of $50. And, of course, this pledge also will be tax-deductible. Is that agreeable?

POTENTIAL CONTRIBUTOR: I don't like to commit to something like this over the phone.

CALLER: I don't blame you. I don't like to, either. But for something as important as the Center, I would make an exception, and I hope you will, too. I'd like to put you down for a pledge of $100. I'll break this into two consecutive monthly installments of $50. This installment plan is designed for people like you: people who understand our needs and would like to make a substantial commitment but who can't do it all at once. How about it?

POTENTIAL CONTRIBUTOR: You're wasting your time. Thank you anyway.

CALLER (quickly): Here, I have it. I found a level that I think is perfect for you: the $50 pledge. Most people I have spoken with this evening have found this level affordable. We also have a gift for you. For a $50 pledge, you'll receive a Community Center coffee mug. How about it?

POTENTIAL CONTRIBUTOR: That's more like it.

These three dialogues have given you an idea of how to negotiate big pledges easily. They are packed with complaints and excuses. Don't worry; rarely will you deal with people as difficult as the potential contributors in these sample dialogues. We want you to know the worst so you will be ready for it.

Twenty Keys to Negotiating

This section analyzes the components of the negotiation process which are embedded in these sample dialogues. Once again, although the dialogues deal with different organizations and the callers come across different problems, you will discover that among the differences are common strands used in all proper negotiations.

1. *Ask for a Specific Dollar Amount*

Control the conversation by asking for specific dollar amounts. This is the most important rule in telephone fund raising and was adhered to strictly in all three dialogues. It is so important that we spell out its corollaries.

1. Never ask the potential contributor, "Can you pledge?" or "Do you want to pledge?" If the potential contributor says no, there is little you can do. But if you ask the potential contributor for a specific dollar amount and he says no, you can always ask him for a more moderate figure instead.

2. Never ask the potential contributor undirected questions such as, "Can you give less?" New callers fall in love with this type of un-directed question. It is so easy. It is so inoffensive. And it is so ineffec-tive. Let's say a caller asks a potential contributor for $200. The potential contributor firmly says no. Next, the caller meekly asks "Can you give less?" or "How about a smaller amount?" The potential contributor will either say no, in which case negotiations are over, or will offer the caller between $5 and $15. What did the caller mean by a smaller amount—$150, $100, $50? What the caller meant is immaterial. What matters is what the potential contributor thinks the caller meant. When a potential contributor hears "small," he thinks really small. Accordingly, do not ask the potential contributor undirected questions such as, "Can you give less?" Rather, ask the potential contributor for a smaller but specific dollar amount. If you ask him for a smaller specific amount and he says no, then ask him for an even smaller specific amount.

3. Never ask the potential contributor what he wants to pledge or what he would feel comfortable giving. To do so is to relinquish control of the conversation. As a telephone fund raiser, you must guide the conver-sation at all times. You do so by asking for specific dollar amounts.

4. Never ask the potential contributor to choose between two pledge amounts. He will chose the smaller amount, of course, if he pledges at all. Once again, be as specific as possible. Asking the poten-

tial contributor to pledge one amount is more specific than offering him a choice of two.

5. And, finally, never offer the potential contributor a range from which he can pledge. He will choose an amount at the low end of the range. Once again, be specific.

2. Use Installments

Installments are an excellent way to make large pledges manageable for your potential contributors. You will notice that they were used in all the dialogues to secure large pledge commitments. For example, in Dialogue 1, the caller says:

> Let's try something more moderate, a gift of $250. You can break this pledge into two installments of $125. That means you will pay $125 now and $125 six months from now.

Do not offer installments after a pledge has been made. It is preferable to get all your money at once. Use installments as a negotiating tool only.

When using installments, offer only one installment possibility at a time. Never offer a potential contributor two installment options at once. For example, do not say, "How about a pledge of $200? You can pay that in two semiannual installments of $100 or in four quarterly installments of $50?" Once again, specificity is rewarded, and one option is more specific than two.

When using installments, it is as important to be clear as it is to be specific. In all three dialogues, the installment option was explained clearly so there could be no confusion. For example, the callers did not ask for $50 quarterly. After all, this could be interpreted as meaning either $50 each quarter or $12.50 each quarter. Rather, the callers asked for a total of $200 to be paid in four quarterly installments of $50. This way there could be no confusion.

If you offer a potential contributor the option of paying a pledge semiannually, he will assume that he is to pay half now and the other half in six months. Likewise, if you offer him the option of paying a pledge quarterly, he will assume he is to pay one fourth now and an additional one fourth every three months. Most programs, by the way, structure their installment option based on these assumptions.

If your program is structured this way, make sure you use the words "quarterly" or "semiannually" or spell out when the payments will fall due. For example, in Dialogue 1, the caller presented the installment option clearly:

You can break this pledge into two installments of $125. *That means you will pay $125 now and $125 six months from now.*

The caller in Dialogue 2 also was clear:

That's why I'm hoping that you can help us with a $300 gift. *You can pay this in quarterly installments of $75 each.*

Of course, there are other ways to structure the installment option. For example, the Community Center in Dialogue 3 designed a monthly payment plan. With this plan, if a potential contributor divides her pledge into two installments, she will pay one half immediately and the other half the following month. If a potential contributor divides her pledge into three installments, she will pay one third immediately, one third the following month, and one third the month after that.

If you choose an untraditional plan like this, make sure it is clear to potential callers. The caller in Dialogue 3 was clear. She always asked that the installments be paid in "consecutive months."

The traditional installment plan is a stronger negotiating tool than is the untraditional plan because it allows potential contributors to spread their payment over an entire year. The less desirable aspect of the traditional installment plan is that you have to wait longer to get your money. Weigh the costs and benefits of each option in light of the needs of your organization to determine which is more appropriate for you.

Although installments are effective negotiating tools, they are time consuming to administer. Also, you only receive a portion of the money immediately. For these reasons, use installments only at the higher levels, and do not break pledges into more than four installments unless you have highly organized clerical help. In that case, you might find even monthly installments feasible.

Finally, if your program needs to collect a set amount of money immediately or if your program is temporary (a one-shot deal), avoid installments. They are better suited for permanent programs with long-range as well as immediate needs.

3. *Break the Pledge Down*

Do not expect potential contributors to do mental arithmetic and figure out that you are not asking for the moon after all. It is your job to break the pledge down into smaller amounts and then equate these amounts to an inexpensive item. Let them know, as the caller did in Dialogue 1, that the amount you are asking for is less per day than the cost of a cup of coffee, for example, or less per week than the cost of a movie.

A smart environmental organization includes in its negotiations a request for just one nickel—for every toxic waste site in the United States. It will take only a short time for you to put together a list of apt, specific breakdowns like this for your organization. You also will need a list of general comparisons. Most of us buy cups of coffee, see movies, read the daily paper, and so on and can easily see meaning in these sorts of simple, general comparisons. Also, do not forget that you can break pledges down per family member.

So a $200 pledge is less than $4 a week, less than the cost of a movie. It is less than 60¢ a day, less than the cost of a bus ride. It is less than 15¢ a day per person in a family of four, less than the cost of a paper.

Breaking pledges down and drawing graphic comparisons were done in all three dialogues. For example, In Dialogue 1, the caller told the potential contributor that a $150 pledge amounts to less than 60¢ a week per family member. In Dialogue 2, the caller told the potential contributor that a $50 pledge amounts to less than $1 a week to insure favorable congressional action. In this case the caller let the potential contributor know that the value of the organization is great while the amount of money asked for is slight.

4. Restate the Specific Dollar Amount

Using installments and breaking down pledges into smaller amounts and then equating these amounts to an inexpensive item are good negotiating tools. But do not let potential contributors lose track of the total pledge request. After you use these tools, finish by discussing the total pledge request. ("How about a $200 pledge, Bob?")

5. Control the Conversation

Ideally, in the negotiating game you make a move, they make a move, and so on. But sometimes the potential contributor makes two moves at once. First he tells you that he cannot afford the level of giving you requested. Then he tells you what he can afford. What do you do now? Do you accept his offer? No. To accept the offer is to lose control of the conversation and to throw away money.

What you should do first is thank him for his offer. Second, explain why you need more. Finally, ask him for more (in the form of a specific dollar amount, of course). This is what the caller did in Dialogue 2 when the potential contributor offered $35. The caller thanked him for the offer but then explained why he needed more money this year—because Congress no longer was representing the views of the organization. He then asked the potential contributor to give the $35 four times throughout the year for a total of $140.

At first, this may seem absurd. The potential contributor tells the caller he can afford only $35, but the caller still asks for $140. Does this jeopardize the $35 offer? Well, it might, but fortune favors the audacious. For every small pledge that you lose, you will pick up a large one. By asking for four times the original offer, you create a great deal of negotiating room. If the potential contributor says no to your new request, you still can ask him for the $35 twice during the year.

Naturally, you will not always ask the person to give you the offered amount four times during the year. Here is where common sense comes in. For example, if you ask the potential contributor for a pledge of $300 and he offers you $100 instead, ask him to give you the $100 semiannually for a total of $200. If the potential contributor says no, you then can ask for $150.

In sum, stay in control of the conversation by asking for specific dollar amounts. If the potential contributor offers you a smaller amount, do not allow this to floor you. Thank him for his offer, explain why you need more and then ask him for more. Using installments is an effective way to do this. Installments bridge the gap between your offer and his response. You are willing to accept his offer. You simply want him to give you that amount three more times, for example, during the year. In other words, listen to him and tailor your request to his response.

There are two additional points to note about staying in control of the conversation. First, do not be afraid to interrupt a long-winded person. Guide the conversation. It should be a dialogue with you in control, not a monologue on either side. You can interrupt politely by saying: "What you are saying is very interesting. But I would like to point out . . . ."

And, second, avoid long pauses. They are deadly. A long pause— five seconds or more—is a hole in your conversation through which the potential contributor can slip away. This is not to say that you should never pause or never let the potential contributor speak. But there must never be gaps in the conversation that let the potential contributor gain control of the conversation.

6. Assume Everyone Can Give

Some callers make unwarranted assumptions about whole groups of people: retired senior citizens, unemployed people, parents of children in college or private school, and teachers, for example. They assume that these people cannot afford to give and therefore they do not pursue hard-line negotiations with them. But these people can give. You have a level of giving that is suited just for them. Remember, all these people, whatever their income level, are going to benefit, some of them enormously, from what your organization does. Make them sense that what they give will make a difference.

While we warn you against making assumptions about who can give, we concede that, as a general rule, some of your assumptions will be accurate. Most senior citizens are not wealthy; neither are most school teachers. Nonetheless, there are exceptions to the rules. Rich people do grow old!

If you proceed on the assumption that a particular potential contributor can make a large contribution and you happen to be wrong, you can adjust your pledge requests downward. Proceeding on the assumption that everyone can give does not cost you anything.

On the other hand, if you assume that a certain person cannot make a large contribution and you turn out to be wrong, there is little you can do to rectify your mistake. The error in assumption is irreversible in almost all instances. For example, if you ask a potential contributor for $100 initially and the potential contributor says yes immediately, it is difficult, if not impossible, to convince him that what you really meant was $300.

A corollary to the rule assuming everyone can give is this directive: never make a negative statement such as, "So you don't want to give?" or "So you can't pledge anything?" New callers sometimes make the fatal mistake of asking potential contributors questions like these. The answer is always a resounding "That's right!"

7. Assume Everyone Wants to Give

Just as you assume that everyone can give, assume that everyone wants to give. Do not make the mistake of assuming that unless a potential contributor is enthusiastic, she is uninterested.

Because you cannot rely on potential contributors for enthusiasm, you must be enthusiastic. Let your enthusiasm be reflected in your voice. Enthusiasm is contagious. If the potential contributor does not think you are excited about your organization, there is little reason for him to be excited about it. If you are excited about it, the potential contributor will become excited as well, even though that may not be reflected in his voice.

Although you must start with the assumption that all potential contributors are interested, sometimes your assumption will be wrong. It is not entirely uncommon for potential contributors to tell you at the beginning of the phone call that they are not interested in your organization. Do not take this as an indication that you should end the call. If a potential contributor tells you she is not interested, try to convince her that her lack of interest would be interest if only she had a little more information—which, of course, you would be happy to provide. Say something like this:

> I have a feeling that if you knew just a little more about us you would share my enthusiasm. I would like to take a few minutes to tell you what we have done and what we intend to do.

Then without a pause begin to tell her what you have done, what you intend to do, and, of course, why her support is important. The emphasis should be on mutual self-interest. Very often potential contributors are uninterested because they do not perceive themselves as benefiting from your program. The importance of emphasizing mutual self-interest is the next rule discussed.

Of course, the approach we recommend for dealing with uninterested potential contributors—providing them with information about your organization, stressing the connection between your goals and their self-interest—does not always work. Sometimes potential contributors will cut you off before you have the opportunity to provide the information. In other cases, despite your efforts, potential contributors will decide not to give.

While the approach does not always work, there is no better alternative. There are only two other alternatives, neither of which is satisfactory.

First, you could thank the potential contributor for her honesty and end the call. The problem with this approach is that you will never get any money. While the recommended approach does not always work, this approach never works. It might save you a little time, but it would cost you a lot of dollars.

Second, you could ignore the potential contributor's comment and continue along. This works occasionally. More often than not, however, the potential contributor will become annoyed with you for ignoring her comment, and will reiterate her feelings and then hang up.

The recommended approach neither antagonizes potential contributors nor surrenders negotiations. Rather, it provides potential contributors with valuable information about your organization and provides callers with the opportunity to get a pledge. If you follow the recommended approach, you will receive pledges from approximately 20% of those who at the outset claimed to have no interest, and your efforts to involve the other 80% will not be wasted. Even if a potential contributor does not pledge, she still knows more about your organization than she did before she was called. She now will follow your organization's activities more closely. She no doubt will be pleased with its performance. And she probably will give the next time she is called.

8. Emphasize Mutual Self-Interest

Virtually never does anyone contribute anything unless self-interest is involved. You must establish a connection between your organization's activities and the potential contributor's self-interest. Do not expect potential contributors to make this connection on their own.

For example, in Dialogue 2, the negotiator frequently made the connection between the organization and the potential contributor. She left nothing to guesswork. For example, early in the call she said:

> Last year, we were able to defeat three bills that would have wiped out *our* political gains of the last decade. We succeeded in protecting your interests.

Later in the call, she said:

> How about that, Ms. Ford? One dollar a week to insure that Congress responds to *our* strong constituency.

In both instances, the caller stressed the word "our." By doing so, she subtly but effectively treated the potential contributor and the organization as one.

In our discussion of Rule 7 (Assume Everyone Wants to Give), we said that you should emphasize mutual self-interest to persuade an uninterested potential contributor to support you. This is because potential contributors frequently are uninterested because they do not see the connection between your interests and theirs. The following is a response to a potential contributor who said he was uninterested. It shows you how to use mutual self-interest to convert lack of interest to interest.

> I have a feeling that if you knew a little more about the Delran Athletic League you would share my enthusiasm and become one of our supporters. As you probably know, we provide organized activities for inner-city children who otherwise would have no structure to their lives during the day. Five years ago, 350 kids were involved in our program. This year, more than 1500 kids are no longer on the streets, but instead are working and growing with us. These kids are good kids. But they're the same kids who a few years ago were constantly at war with the law. As citizens of Delran, we all have an interest not only in helping those who are less fortunate than ourselves, but also in helping ourselves by making our city

as safe as possible. The D.A.L. goes a long way toward achieving both of these goals. That's why I hope you can join the D.A.L. this evening with a pledge of $250. (Notice how the caller immediately starts negotiating after dealing with the potential contributor's initial lack of interest.)

9. Make Friends with the Potential Contributor

People do not give to causes; people give to people. This old chestnut has been around so long because it is true. Make friends with the potential contributor. If he likes you, he is more likely to give money to you. Personalize the call as you would with a friend. You can:

1. Interject the potential contributor's name now and then into the conversation. This lets him know that you are not following a standard pitch. It lets him know that you are dealing with him on a one-to-one basis. It is a simple but nice touch. His response when you ask for him at the very beginning of the call may indicate how you should address him. For example, if you ask for Fred Hayes and the potential contributor answers, "This is Fred," call him Fred throughout the call. If you ask for Fred Hayes, and the potential contributor answers, "This is Mr. Hayes," call him Mr. Hayes throughout the call.

2. Keep your language casual. Avoid multisyllabic words or complex sentence structure. Use the same words, expressions, and grammatical patterns that you would use with a friend.

3. During negotiations, use information you pick up during the call about the potential contributor. For example, in Dialogue 1, the potential contributor told the caller that he has a family of five. When the caller asked him for a $150 pledge, he used this information by letting the potential contributor know that this pledge is less than 60¢ per week per family member. In Dialogue 2, the potential contributor told the caller her main concern is lobbying. Throughout the call, the caller emphasized the importance of the organization's lobbying efforts.

4. Let the potential contributor know that you will design the pledge to meet his needs. In Dialogue 1, the caller told the potential contributor that he will break the $150 pledge into four installments to make payment as comfortable as possible for him. In Dialogue 3, the caller told the potential contributor that he has an installment plan designed specially for people like him.

5. Make the potential contributor feel good about his pledge. Do this by telling him how important he really is to your organization and how significant his gift will be. In Dialogue 3, the caller did this outright

when she told the potential contributor, "This truly is our make-or-break year, and I hope you will help us make it."

10. Assuage Irritated Potential Contributors

Sometimes a potential contributor will become irritated as a result of your persistent pledge requests. This may be because you were over-zealous in your pursuit of a pledge. Or it may be because the potential contributor is particularly sensitive. Irrespective of the cause of the potential contributor's irritation, it is the caller's job to assuage it. An agitated potential contributor does not give.

Confront the issue head on. Let the potential contributor know that you realize she is irritated, apologize for your actions, and then explain your behavior. This is what happened in Dialogue 3. The potential contributor made it known that he felt pressured. The negotiator reponded: "I don't mean to pressure you. It's just that I'm very enthusiastic about the community center. If you were here, you would share my enthusiasm."

Should you ever attempt to assuage a potential contributor when you think that she is agitated, even if she does not say so? Yes, but use apologies sparingly. Do not get in the habit of apologizing for your actions. After all, you represent a worthy cause and are trying to find a way for the potential contributor to support it with as little strain as possible. Only apologize if you think that the potential contributor feels that you are working against her rather than with her. Say something like this: "I hope you don't think I'm trying to pressure you. I know it may sound that way. It's just that I am very excited about our future. And I'm really hoping that you'll become a part of it."

11. Emphasize the Tax Benefits

Favorable tax consequences attach to charitable giving. A contribution today will save the potential contributor money when his taxes comes due. It is in the interest of both you and the potential contributor if you remind him about this, as the callers did in Dialogues 1 and 3. Emphasizing tax benefits is a way of emphasizing mutual self-interest. The caller did not mention favorable tax consequences in Dialogue 2 because contributions to political organizations usually do not yield favorable tax consequences.

Emphasize the favorable tax consequences—that a contribution to your organization is tax-deductible, for example—especially at the higher levels of giving. As a general rule, the larger the gift, the greater the tax savings.

Tax savings are particularly important at the end of the year. Many taxpapers are told by their accountants in October and November how much money they need to give away. Therefore, telephone fund raising flourishes in December. Most taxpapers expect to give money to some organization, but which one? Your call solves their dilemma. Therefore, push tax savings most heavily in December. Because December is such a productive month for telephone fund raising, if you are planning a one-shot deal, schedule it for December, if possible.

Because the tax code changes constantly, we cannot provide you with the tax rules. Nonetheless, it is likely that charitable giving always will receive some special treatment under the Internal Revenue Code.

12. Stress Timing

Convince potential contributors that the moment they speak with you is the moment to give. To do so, you need to demonstrate a particular need that can be met only if you receive support immediately. The following illustrates this:

CALLER: Can I put you down for a $150 pledge?
POTENTIAL CONTRIBUTOR: I'll have to think about it. I also would like to give some money to the United Way and to my church.
CALLER: Well, if at all possible, I would like to arrive at some commitment this evening. As you may know, we have been severely hurt by recent cuts in the amount of funding that we get from the state. We are negotiating right now to have that funding reinstated. We need your commitment now. The amount of money we get from the state depends upon the amount of money we get from our community. That's why I want to put you down for a pledge this evening. How about a $100 pledge? If you decide to give more, naturally that would be great. But for now, at least we could count on you for $100. And. . . .

If your program is a one-shot deal, emphasize the one-time nature of your program. It is now or never! Of course, explain what prompted you to institute the fund-raising campaign.

If you are doing political fund raising, timing may be your strongest argument. For example, during a presidential campaign you might argue, "If we don't win this primary, there won't be another one. That's why we really need your support now." Or, during a legislative battle you might argue, "If we don't stop this bill from passing, any support that you subsequently might give will be too late."

Other times when you can conveniently stress the need for an immediate pledge are: (1) at the end of the calendar year, which, of course, is meaningful to potential contributors for tax reasons; (2) at the end of your organization's fiscal year; (3) when you need money to put on a special event or production; (4) if an emergency of any kind comes up and you need to be rescued by your local supporters; and (5) in order to meet a deadline for matching funds.

13. Emphasize That the Money Will Go for the Purpose Intended

People often fear that the money they contribute to worthy causes ends up paying for inflated salaries and the like. Make it clear to potential contributors that the money they give you will go to further one of the purposes for which the organization was created. For example, if you are an art museum, tell the potential contributor that his contribution "will go directly into the fund for the purchase of new paintings," as the caller did in Dialogue 1.

On the other hand, non-profit-making organizations, like other businesses, need to budget money for overhead. It takes money to raise money. These are called fund-raising expenses. And it takes money to spend money. These are called management expenses. Naturally, non-profits cannot reduce overhead to zero, but overhead should be reasonable and in proper relation to money spent on projects that are dear to the hearts of contributors. It is a good idea for nonprofits to make their budgets available on request, so contributors can see for themselves that they are not paying for unproductive fund-raising methods or wasteful management. A warning: If overhead goes up over 30%, contributors are likely to ask questions. There may be legitimate answers to those questions. Callers must be able to express those answers lucidly.

14. Speak Only with the Potential Contributor

Even though it sometimes is tempting to just go ahead and talk to whoever answers the phone when you call, do not give in to temptation. Always save your time and energy for the potential contributor himself, the person whose name you have before you on the potential contributor record (which you will learn about later). For one thing, it is the potential contributor who will have received a postcard from your organization announcing your call (which you also will learn about later). But more important, another member of the household rarely will negotiate seriously. When the talk turns to money, she probably will suggest that she pass on your message to the potential contributor. If you agree to this, be prepared to get a refusal when you call back. When you speak directly to a potential contributor, you can ask for specific dollar amounts, use installments, break the pledge down, control the conversation, and so on, as you are learning to do. Someone relaying your message secondhand will have neither the interest nor the ability to do these things. Her conversation with the potential contributor most likely will be blunt: "(Name of your organization) called today. They need money. Want to give them any this year?"

Or, the person to whom you speak may simply refuse to pledge. Result: a wasted potential contributor. Giving it another try by calling back later and insisting on talking with the potential contributor usually will do absolutely no good.

It is particularly tough to get past spouses of potential contributors, who may insist that decisions about money are made jointly. To get around them adroitly, explain that personally you would be glad to speak with them, but you have instructions from your organization to speak only with the potential contributor herself.

There is one exception to the rule about speaking only with the potential contributor. If the potential contributor is deceased, treat the spouse as the potential contributor.

15. Avoid Call Backs

Once you have the potential contributor on the phone, do not let him talk you into calling him back later. Potential contributors frequently ask to be called back when they do not want to make a commitment that evening. The potential contributor often will say that he needs time to think over the pledge. It is better to get a moderate pledge from him on Monday than it is to hope for a large pledge on Thursday. Between Monday and Thursday, the potential contributor might be called by another, more persistent organization and decide to give money to it. He might receive a large bill and temporarily reconsider any charitable giving. Or he might just have a bad day and not be in a philanthropic mood when you speak with him that evening. When you have invested time with a potential contributor, try to get him to make a commitment that evening.

Avoid call backs by convincing the potential contributor to commit to an amount slightly lower than you think he can give. This happened in Dialogue 1. The potential contributor wanted to be called back a week later so he could think over a $150 pledge. The caller explained why it was important to arrive at a figure that evening: the commitment was essential because the museum was negotiating for matching funds from the government. He then asked the potential contributor for a $100 pledge.

Other arguments can be equally persuasive. You might mention that his commitment that evening is important so that your group can determine its annual budget. You might mention a specific need that warrants his pledge immediately. An emergency has arisen, for example, and you need funds to set things right.

After you have explained to the potential contributor why you need his commitment immediately, do not wait for him to say that he understands. As in Dialogue 1, quickly return to negotiations and ask for a specific amount of money. Ask him for an amount slightly lower than the prior amount. You are asking him to compromise; it is expedient for you to do the same.

16. Pursue Credit Card Pledges

Credit card pledges are the best pledges. After you have taken down the potential contributor's credit card number and its expiration date, the pledge is no longer a pledge. Rather, it is money in the bank; the transaction is complete.

The credit card company will keep a percentage of each pledge. This percentage is small in comparison to the cost of pledge collection, as you will learn later.

The credit card pledge also removes some anxiety from your program. You do not have to wait for the pledge to come in; you already have it. Rarely does anyone reconsider a credit card pledge. If the person gives you his credit card number over the phone, he invariably will honor the commitment.

Finally, using his credit card gives the potential contributor a cushion in case of financial hardship. This, of course, benefits you. If he has a financial problem, he probably will not back out of his pledge but instead will space out his payments on his credit card.

Do not take credit card pledges for one-shot deals. The difficulty of establishing a credit card system for your one-shot deal outweighs the advantages.

17. Do Not Argue with Potential Contributors; Recognize the Validity of Their Complaint

Philosophical foes are potential contributors who are philosophically opposed to what you are doing: you are a prolife group and the potential contributor is prochoice, for example, or you are working for a liberal candidate and the potential contributor is a conservative. If time were free and you had all the time in the world, it would be worth trying to bring philosophical foes over to your side. But time is money and you have a limited amount of both, so do not try to persuade philosophical foes to join your ranks. In most cases, your efforts will fail. Instead, abruptly but politely terminate the call as soon as you discover that the potential contributor is philosophically opposed to your group. Say something like this: "I'm sorry to have bothered you. Have a good evening."

Warning: There are fewer philosophical foes than you might expect. Few people are philosophically opposed to art museums, educational institutions, theatre groups, and the like. The only organizations that will encounter a significant number of philosophical foes are political or issue-oriented organizations.

In most cases, dissatisfied potential contributors are philosophically behind you, but object to a particular person, policy, or program. These people often are very impassioned. They are frustrated. They would like to support you, but there is an obstacle to their doing so. Although they probably would not admit it, they want to remove the obstacle as much as you do.

In Dialogue 2, the potential contributor voiced a particular complaint: she objected to the organization's hiring of Charles Lind. (Charles Lind was the lobbyist who was hired by the political action group and who was subsequently let go.) Let's examine the caller's response to see what steps she took to deal with the problem.:

> CALLER: I can understand your being angry that we hired Charles Lind. It was a mistake on our part, and we publicly apologized. I hope you realize that he no longer works for us and that we intend to be more selective in future hiring. Please accept my apologies on behalf of the organization. While we did make a mistake in hiring Charles Lind, we have made wonderful progress in other areas. For example, last year we were able to defeat three bills that would have wiped out our political gains of the last decade. We succeeded in protecting your interests. That's why I'm hoping you can help us with a $300 gift.

The caller dealt with the complaint by first recognizing the validity of the potential contributor's complaint. Remember, there are two points of views, yours and theirs. Their point is usually valid (at least they think so), so do not argue with them. Moreover, arguing with a potential contributor will only aggravate him, and an aggravated potential contributor does not pledge. Second, the caller explained the organization's position: corrective measures were taken; Charles Lind was let go. And third, the caller asked for money.

Let's apply this three-step approach to another possible complaint: the potential contributor objects to being called at home. First, recognize the validity of the complaint. Let the potential contributor know that you do not like being called at home either, but that you would make an exception for a cause as worthy as yours. Second, apologize for the inconvenience. But then justify your position. Explain why it is important to call: your organization needs money. Then ask for the money.

Another possible complaint: the potential contributor did not receive the premium (the gift) he was promised when he pledged last year. (Premiums are discussed later.) As you will see in the response to this complaint which follows, the caller apologizes briefly, explains what caused the mishap and assures the potential contributor that she personally will see to it that his premium is sent out the next day. She also reminds the potential contributor about what he did receive: the services of the organization. Then she asks for money.

> CALLER: You certainly have a right to be angry, but the truth is that we had such an overwhelming response to our appeal that we got considerably behind in sending out the premiums. We are pleased about the overwhelming response, of course, but we are embarrassed about not getting the premiums out promptly, especially to good friends like yourself. I am relieved that you and I have talked so that I can put things right. But, you know, in a very real sense you did receive a premium and that was superbly programmed classical music 24 hours a day. You certainly can't find that on any other radio station in Omaha. Isn't that worth giving us a second chance to prove that we can come through both with delightful programming and your premium? A contribution of $250 will help insure that we can continue our programming totally without interruption by commercial messages. How about a contribution of $250?

If you are doing political fund raising, your candidate or organization will be taking positions on a myriad of issues and invariably some of these positions will displease some of your potential contributors. But do not despair. It is not necessary that a potential contributor agree with you on every issue. The three-step approach will work well for you, especially if you emphasize those issues on which you do agree.

Two warnings: first, occasionally there will be a potential contributor who does not really care about your organization and does not have any intention of giving, yet presents you with reason after reason for not giving rather than simply telling you that she is not interested. If you sense that the potential contributor is argumentative and not genuinely interested, terminate the call. But do not rudely hang up. Instead, say something like this:

> I have been taking note of your comments. I appreciate your input. I will pass it on to the appropriate person. Thank you for your time.

Second, some potential contributors who are interested in your organization are nonetheless argumentative. Being argumentative and being interested are not mutually exclusive. If after you discuss a particular issue with a potential contributor you sense she is not entirely satisfied with your response yet is interested in your organization, say something like this:

> I think you have made some excellent points. And I assure you that I will pass them on to the appropriate person. While you may not completely approve of our decision to eliminate soccer as an extracurricular activity, I suspect that you still support most of what we've done and approve of what we intend to do. I hope, because of your overall support for our organization, that you'll consider a pledge this evening of $250.

This type of response lets the potential contributor know that it's time to move on to accomplish the purpose of the call—getting a pledge—without making her feel that you disregarded her sentiments.

A note to directors: after your organization has been doing telephone fund raising for a while, you will find that certain complaints arise frequently. List these complaints along with a prepared response for each one and give them to each of your callers to use while negotiating. A sample follows on page 23. As you can see, the first three complaints are general. They could apply to any organization. The fourth complaint is specific to the organization. But, the approach used to handle it applies universally.

18. Do Not Belittle Other Charitable Organizations; Stress the Value of Your Own

There are potential contributors who will be impressed with your organization. They will appreciate your goals and approve of your programs. And they will tell you that if they were rich they would happily support you, but, as it is, they cannot. They have other giving priorities. You are good but not good enough.

What do you do to convince a potential contributor that you are as good as, if not better than, his stated preference? Emphasize the merits of your organization. Stress the connection between your organization

Common Problems

When they say:	You say:
1. I don't like to make a commitment about money over the phone/I don't like being called at home.	Quite frankly, I don't like it either. But for something as important as the Community Center I would make an exception, and I hope that you will, too. That's why I was hoping you could support us this evening with a pledge of $ _____.
2. Mail me some information and I'll think it over.	I'm sorry (potential contributor's name), but I don't have any information I can mail you, but I do have a pledge form in front of me, and I would like to fill it out so that I can mail it to you tomorrow. Anything you need to know I can tell you.
3. I never receive any mail from the Center other than requests for money.	Unfortunately, we had a problem with our records, and some people have not been receiving our (newsletter, announcements of special events, etc.). Let me check your address so that I can make sure we have your correct address on our permanent files. You should begin to receive our (newsletter, announcements of special events, etc.) regularly. (Check address.) Now that we have that taken care of, I'd like to talk to you about how you can make an extra special commitment this evening. For a pledge of $ _____. . . .
4. You should not have cut out your free summer program for latchkey children.	You're not the only one, (potential contributor's name), who wishes we had not cut out that program. It was one of the most difficult decisions we ever made. Unfortunately, our financial condition left us no choice. You'll be happy to hear, however, that we hope to reinstate the program next summer. Strong community support from people like you can help us do that with a pledge this evening of $ _____.

and his self-interest. Point out the importance of the timing of your appeal. These techniques should not be new to you. They are part of all negotiations. But they are particularly important in situations like this. The following example is illustrative:

> CALLER: How about a pledge of $200, Ed? Here at the college we are really counting on your support.
>
> POTENTIAL CONTRIBUTOR: I hate to say no, because every year I realize more and more what the school did for me. But say no I must. I have pledged to my limit and beyond so my church can build a new wing.
>
> CALLER: Congratulations! It does my heart good to talk to a man who realizes that contributions from the private sector often are necessary to accomplish worthwhile goals. We, like your church, also need help. This year we intend to double our computer facilities. Our goal is to have one computer for every ten students. At the same time, we are expanding the library. We need your support for both of these important projects. Could you help us with a gift of $250?

While it is okay to suggest that your organization is more worthy or more needy by emphasizing your merits or your needs, never explicitly state that the potential contributor's other giving priorities are less worthy or less needy. You will notice in the prior example that the caller did not suggest that the potential contributor should not give to his church, but rather that he should give to his alma mater as well. There is a big difference between tooting your own horn and bad-mouthing the opposition, as one coach from a college athletic team learned. The coach was trying to raise funds from former team players to send his current team to Europe to compete in an international tournament. One potential contributor told him that he intended to pledge $500 to the American Cancer Society and therefore could not make a substantial gift to the team. Rather than stressing the importance and one-time nature of the tournament, the coach suggested that the gift to the American Cancer Society was not as important. He told the potential contributor that $500 was nothing to the American Cancer Society, but a pledge of $200 to the team would be the difference between competing and not competing. The potential contributor was outraged, since his son had recently died of cancer. Not only was the pledge lost, so was a long-time friend of the team.

19. Use Clubs

As Dialogue 1 demonstrates, clubs can be valuable negotiating tools. They provide potential contributors with one more incentive to give.

Clubs serve two purposes. First, everyone likes to feel important. Being invited to join a club that is not open to everyone makes one feel important. Second, almost everyone likes to be part of a group. Clubs give people a chance to become part of a group. Because clubs appeal to these two human instincts, they are an effective negotiating tool that can make a substantial level of giving more attractive. The following excerpt from Dialogue 1 is an example of how clubs can be integrated into pledge negotiations:

> Let's try something more moderate, a gift of $250. You can break this pledge into two installments of $125. That means that you will pay $125 now and $125 six months from now. That will make you a member of the Creative Circle. As a member of the Creative Circle, you'll receive invitations to advance private showings of exhibits and to all our other special events. In addition, you will receive a pass entitling you and the other members of your family to free admission. And, of course, this gift will be tax-deductible. How about that, Dave? For less than $1 a day, you can become a member of the Creative Circle.

Clubs can be particularly helpful when you want to upgrade a pledge; in other words, when the potential contributor offers you a small pledge. The following dialogue is instructive:

> CALLER: And that pledge works out to less than $3 a week. How about it, Mr. Grey? How about a pledge of $150?
> POTENTIAL CONTRIBUTOR: No way. Listen, you're still asking me for the world. I'll tell you what I'll do, though. I'll send you a check for $50.
> CALLER: That's terrific! Could you send us that $50 now and then again in six months? That would be a total of $100. And that would make you a member of the Providers Club. Here at the hospital we decided to create a special association for the supporters who are directly responsible for helping us maintain our high standard of care. Twice a year we meet with the Providers Club to discuss how we can provide better service to the community. You see, Mr. Grey, we want your ideas as well as your money. Can we count on you for a $100 pledge?

If clubs can be so helpful, why weren't they used in all three dialogues? Why were clubs only used by one of the three organizations? The answer is that clubs can be complicated to administer and costly. Therefore, not all organizations choose to use them. In Chapter 4, we discuss the pros and cons of using clubs, as well as how to decide whether or not to use them at all, and, if so, how many clubs to have, what their names should be, which benefits should attach to each one, and so on. But the important point for this section is simply to understand that clubs are like any other negotiating tool: they are a device that makes charitable giving more appealing.

20. Use Premiums

Premiums, like clubs, can be valuable negotiating tools providing potential contributors with one or more incentives to give—and every little incentive helps. A premium is an appealing item, usually inexpensive, that reminds the contributor and others of your group and that the contributor finds useful.

Everyone likes to feel important, and receiving a special gift makes one feel important. In addition, just as clubs appeal to that something in us that makes us want to belong, premiums appeal to that something in us that makes us want to let everyone know that we belong. As you will learn, premiums—tote bags, shirts, bumper stickers, and the like—usually display the logo or some other reminder of your organization. When contributors use them, they declare to the world that they are generous people who are willing to support a cause they believe in. Finally, premiums let contributors know that the good feelings are mutual. You like them as much as they like you, and you are willing to send them a token of your affection, something for them to remember you by. Of course, the most important premiums you offer are the services of your organization. It is good to remind potential contributors of this. Sometimes it is forgotten in the fervor of negotiations.

The following example from Dialogue 3 illustrates how premiums can be integrated into pledge negotiations.

> CALLER: Let's try something more moderate, a gift of $150. You can pay this in three consecutive monthly installments of $50. As you know, Mr. Peters, this pledge is less than $3 a week, and, as our way of saying thank you, we'll send you a Community Center travel bag. I have one, and it's terrific! By the way, this contribution also will be tax-deductible.

Premiums, like clubs, are especially helpful when a potential contributor has offered a small pledge and you are negotiating hard for a more sizeable gift. The following dialogue shows you how to do this. The caller has been negotiating carefully, going down in steps from $500 to $300 to $250. At that point, the potential contributor responded rather abruptly with an offer of $50:

> CALLER: Thanks, Jim, for your offer of $50. That will help the Legion make its outing for the hospitalized vets the success it always has been. But I wonder if you could possibly make that $150. (No pause for his answer.) As a vet yourself, I know you can appreciate how much this outing means to the men in the hospital. We don't want to leave out a single vet.

POTENTIAL CONTRIBUTOR: Sure, I appreciate that. But appreciating it and being able to do something about it are two different things. $50 is my limit this year. My daughter is getting married next month, and she's always after the old man for one thing or another.

CALLER: Let me ask you this. Are you a Rockets fan?

POTENTIAL CONTRIBUTOR: You're darn right I am. Especially when they make up their minds to play ball like they did last week.

CALLER: Then you would enjoy the premium you get for a $150 contribution—two tickets to a Rockets game.

POTENTIAL CONTRIBUTOR: Well . . .

CALLER: For $150 the vets will have a great time at their outing, and you and a friend will have a great time at the game, Jim. It's a win–win situation. How about it?

POTENTIAL CONTRIBUTOR: It's a heck of a lot of money just now. But . . . okay, it's a deal.

CALLER: Thanks, Jim. I'm going to call the Legion Commander right now and tell him about it!

After thanking Jim for his initial offer, the negotiator immediately came back with a request for a considerably higher contribution, but made it palatable by personalizing it. The negotiator correctly emphasized that coming through with $150 would give Jim a great deal of satisfaction as a veteran. But it was that little gift of two tickets to a Rockets game that turned Jim's maybe into yes.

If premiums are helpful, why aren't they used in all three dialogues? Like clubs, premiums can be complicated to administer as well as costly. That is why not all organizations use them. In Chapter 4, we discuss the pros and cons of using premiums, as well as how to decide whether or not to use them at all, and, if so, which kinds work best, and so on. The important point to remember now is that premiums are like any other negotiating tool: they are a device that makes charitable giving more appealing.

Conclusion

Before long, using these twenty rules, as complex as they may seem now, will become second nature. Once you begin to do telephone fund raising, you will be surprised how quickly things fall into place.

What we have written is nothing more than common sense coupled with experience. You have the common sense. Soon you will have the experience and with that a mastery of these rules.

Despite these words of encouragement, there are probably a few of you who would prefer mastering the rules before continuing on. It is impossible to master them without practice. But even without practice, your understanding of them will deepen as you read on. The rules are constantly reexamined and illustrated throughout the book.

Negotiating Tactics to Avoid

Up until now, we have told you how to negotiate affirmatively. We have explored specific techniques that we encourage you to use for successful negotiating. Now we discuss negotiating tactics to avoid. Some may seem tempting. Do not give in. Some negotiators, in their eagerness to garner support for their organization, give in to temptation and find out to their chagrin that the following techniques backfire. Instead of garnering support, they tarnish the image of the organization and cost thousands of dollars in unpledged money.

1. While you should present the organization in its most favorable light, you also have an obligation to be truthful. For example, do not tell Helen Smith, to encourage her support, that half her neighbors gave you money, unless of course it is true. Do not tell Hal Jones that he is one of a select group you decided to call when in reality you are calling everyone in his neighborhood. Do not tell Douglas White that if you do not raise $10,000 immediately your organization will cease to exist when in fact you have $100,000 in reserve.

You will be surprised at how quickly these lies come back to haunt you. It will not be long before the potential contributors, and possibly the press, discover the truth. While lying may bring in a few extra dollars in the short run, ultimately it will cost you dearly. Lying is not only unethical, but also unproductive.

2. Do not change your name to correspond to the ethnic background of the potential contributor. While this may be effective, it is unethical. For example, do not give your name as Greta Gundersen when you are on the line with Mrs. Hansen and then give your name as Bridget Reilley when you are on the line with Mr. O'Rourke. A notorious instance took place when callers with the obvious ethnic accent of their own group claimed—with phony sincerity—to be members of another group. The result was ludicrous, except for the callers themselves, who raised hackles, not money.

A note to directors: While it is unacceptable for a caller to change his name to meet each occasion, it is acceptable for a caller uniformly to announce himself using a name other than his legal name. For example, callers with long, hard-to-pronounce last names often prefer to use short, easy to pronounce last names. Allow them to do so if they notify you of their decision. You must be able to trace each pledge to an identifiable caller.

3. Do not claim you are a volunteer when you are getting paid. It is not uncommon for potential contributors to ask about this. Some callers believe that if they tell potential contributors the truth, it will diminish their ability to negotiate. Not so. Professionalism is always respected. In nine out of ten cases, the person with whom you are speaking works hard and will appreciate that you do the same.

4. Do not lie about your calling location. Some callers tell potential contributors that they are calling from cities other than the one they are actually sitting in. Washington, DC is a favorite, of course. They hope these tactics will even get a potential contributor away from his evening meal, if necessary, and to the phone to receive a call from someone at the hub of power.

5. Do not use sexuality to get pledges. Our society never has looked upon sex in return for money with respect. We once heard a caller say: "Oh, come on, Jeff, You can come up with a little $250 pledge for me, can't you? A guy with a sexy voice like you should not have a problem getting your pledge up." We immediately spoke to the caller. She swore that she had never done it before and would never do it again. But the next day we heard the following: "And you know, Mr. Stevens, if you pledge $200 this evening you'll get a wonderful premium. And the best thing about it is I'll personally deliver it." That was the caller's final call.

In sum, the best advice is to keep credible, and let the worth of your cause do the work, not shady tactics. Telephone fund raisers need to be imaginative and persistent. But more than that, they need to be ethical.

Telephone Style

In the previous section, we discussed negotiating tactics to avoid. In this section, we discuss attitudes, mannerisms, and behaviors to avoid.

1. Do not eat, drink, or smoke while on the phone. This is just too casual and will not impress potential contributors one bit. Remember,

you are a representative of the organization and are conducting business on its behalf. Act with the requisite dignity.

A note to directors: it is okay for callers to have snacks and cigarettes in the calling room. But if you discover that callers abuse the privilege, discontinue it.

2. Do not use profanity. The reason for this rule is obvious: the use of profanity in a professional context is objectionable. This rule applies even if the potential contributor himself uses profane language.

3. Do not meet hostility with hostility. It is dismaying to meet with resentment on the other end of the line, but to be fair to potential contributors, even to grouchy ones, callers should consider their own responses when they are called—in other words, when the shoe is on the other foot, and they become potential contributors. How relaxing is it to listen to an appeal after working hard all day? Are they ever tempted to slam down the receiver abruptly? Like everyone else, of course, their response on the phone differs according to their interests.

4. Do not use sexist language. In the previous section we cautioned against using sexuality intentionally as a way to raise funds. Now, we caution against unintentionally using sexist words, such as "honey" or "doll." You do not intend to offend potential contributors, but you may. Offended potential contributors rarely give.

The Introduction to Negotiating

Now you know how to negotiate large dollar commitments from your supporters. You know what to do and what not to do. You are confident that everyone you call can give a minimum of $50. You cannot call someone and bluntly begin to negotiate, however. You need a friendly introduction.

First, introduce yourself and give the name of the organization you represent. Second, ask to speak to the potential contributor whose name you have before you. Of course, you already have taken a few seconds to figure out how her name is pronounced. Some people, even those with hard to pronounce names, take offense when their names are garbled. If you are uncertain about the pronunciation, ask the director, the supervisor, or as a last resort, the potential contributor herself, proceeding like this:

CALLER: Hello, this is Greg Lewis from the Delaware County Camping and Hiking Club, Mrs. Zmiewski. I believe I am pronouncing your name correctly.

The caller lets the potential contributor know that he is concerned about giving her name the correct pronunciation, but he does not let that slow down the process of making friends during the all-important introduction to negotiations. He is not rattling on at such a great rate that if he has mispronounced her name, the potential contributor cannot break in and tell him so. The flow goes like this. "I believe I am pronouncing your name correctly (one second pause). I'd like to talk with you for a few minutes about the Camping and Hiking Club. We believe clean campsites and well-maintained trails are important to all of us who love the outdoors. . . ."

Third, assure potential contributors, as this caller did, that you will take only a few minutes of their time. Do not ask if you can talk with them. Tell them you would like to talk with them and then, without any pause, go ahead and do it.

Fourth, tell potential contributors as briefly as possible what your organization does and why you need their support.

When you have completed these four steps, begin negotiations. The introduction is short. Potential contributors will give you a limited amount of their precious time. Do not waste it talking about fluff.

As important as what is in the introduction is what is not in the introduction.

1. Do not be guilty of asking the unctuous question, "How are you tonight?" While you intend to be courteous, your question well may anger potential contributors. No matter how sincere you sound, this question obviously is self-serving.

2. Your call will not be cold. Every potential contributor will receive a postcard before she is called. The postcard will alert potential contributors to your impending call. (In chapter 3, we discuss the postcard in detail.) There is no need to mention the postcard during the call, since its basic purpose is to alert potential contributors to the call.

3. Do not waste time asking potential contributors choice questions or open-ended questions. Because asking for money is not easy, callers like to postpone it. In an attempt to defer negotiations and to include potential contributors in the conversation, callers sometimes ask choice questions or open-ended questions. For example, a caller from a public broadcasting station might ask, "Which of our programs is your favorite?" or "What do you think of our objectives?"

There are four problems with this:

• It postpones negotiations, as the nervous caller intended it to do. Potential contributors have a limited amount of time. The more time that is spent on the introduction, the less there is for negotiations.

• Asking potential contributors a question in the introduction surrenders control. For example, a potential contributor may seize on that
question to divert the conversation away from negotiations entirely.
• You may receive exactly what you do not want, a negative response. Some potential contributors will know little or nothing about
your organization or even your cause and so may respond negatively.
For example, potential contributors to a public broadcasting station may
not have a favorite program and may not be interested in the station's
objectives. In addition, it is easier to say no than yes, because yes opens
up possibilities for involvement, and potential contributors know that.
• It uses up the caller's energy and time.

The Pledge Validation

You have a beginning and a middle. Now you need an end. This is
the easiest part of the call. But, just because it seems so easy, callers
sometimes are tempted to skip it and rush right on to the next call.

Actually, the ending—the pledge validation—is the most important
part of the call. The validation has six parts. Ignore none of them.

1. Thank the potential contributor generously for his pledge. When
you thank him, mention the amount he is pledging and the date it is
due: two weeks after the pledge is made. If this pledge is broken into
installments, mention the installments. You might even tell him the
months in which the installments will fall due.

2. Check his address, including the zip code. Without a proper
address, your work will go for naught.

3. Let him know this is a firm commitment on his part and you are
counting on his support. Nothing is more disconcerting than pledges
that are not honored. People who are not sincere about the commitment
might back out at this point in the conversation. So much the better. You
have not yet spent much money or time on them. There is no point
chasing people who do not intend to honor their commitments.

4. Ask him if he or his spouse works for a matching gift company.
Many companies, large corporations in particular, match or even double
their employees' contributions to certain organizations. Ask him to
check on this. By doing so, he may increase the value of his contribution
considerably. But do not mention matching gift companies during negotiations, for this might encourage a potential contributor to decrease the
size of his own gift, anticipating that his employer will make up the
difference.

Do not bother to prepare a list of matching gift companies to which your caller can refer. It is impossible to keep such a list up-to-date.

5. Now ask him for one more favor. This one will not cost him a penny. Ask him for the names and phone numbers of his like-minded friends. Let him know that, if he wishes, you will not use his name when you call. Of course, you hope you can use his name. After all, you are not asking him for confidential information. You simply are asking for the chance to involve his friends in an organization that he obviously believes in.

6. Finally, you want your last words to be a final validation of the commitment. So, once again, thank the contributor profusely—with real feeling in your voice—for his pledge of $_____. Let him know that the next day you will be sending him a validation of his pledge and along with it a prepaid envelope so that he can mail you his check with no trouble. Ask him to return the validation with his check. This simplifies your record-keeping. If your organization is using credit cards, be sure, at this point, to write down the name of the card, the number and the expiration date carefully. The last thing the contributor should hear is the amount of his commitment: "Thank you again, (potential contributor's name), for your $____ pledge."

A note to directors: although pledges normally are due two weeks after they are made, occasionally extending the due date is the wise thing to do. For example, if a potential contributor says that he is short of cash but expects his cash flow to improve the following month, deferring the due date an additional two weeks makes sense. His pledge, then, would not be due until one month after he makes it.

While deferred due dates can be used appropriately, more often than not they are abused. Callers quickly learn that it is easier for potential contributors to agree to a large pledge when the date of payment is comfortably in the future. Shortly after callers learn this, deferring the due date becomes the rule instead of the exception. These deferred pledges are weak, and frequently do not come in.

Because unrestricted use of deferred due dates can hurt your program, we recommend that you do not allow them except under these restrictions:

1. The potential contributor requests the deferral. Without this requirement, there would be no limit to the use of deferred due dates.
2. The length of the deferral is reasonable. What is reasonable will vary with the circumstances.

3. The caller obtains your permission. This alone will limit the use of deferred due dates to legitimate situations.

Review

Before we put everything together in the form of a script, it is time for you to discover how much you have learned. Three dialogues follow. They are loaded with problems. As you read each dialogue, take note of the negotiating weaknesses as you come across them. After each dialogue, we examine the negotiating strengths and weaknesses contained therein. Compare our evaluation with yours.

Dialogue 1

CALLER: Hello, this is Martin Ericson calling from the Newtown Science Foundation. I am calling for Steven Pines.

POTENTIAL CONTRIBUTOR: This is he.

CALLER: May I take a moment of your time?

POTENTIAL CONTRIBUTOR: I'm really busy. I only have a minute.

CALLER: Well, I promise I'll be quick. I'd like to speak with you about the Newtown Science Foundation. As you may know, last year we provided scholarships to five area high school students so they could study at local universities. This year we hope to do the same for eight students. We can only do this with strong community support. Have you supported us in the past?

POTENTIAL CONTRIBUTOR: No, I haven't.

CALLER: Well, maybe this year you could. For example, how about a pledge of $500? Naturally, this gift would be tax-deductible. And you could pay it in installments.

POTENTIAL CONTRIBUTOR: No. I really have to go.

CALLER: Well, how about a pledge of $50 quarterly? Is that more reasonable?

POTENTIAL CONTRIBUTOR: Send me a form. I'll think about it.

CALLER: Well, can I put you down for the $50 quarterly now? Your commitment this evening will help us more than you know.

POTENTIAL CONTRIBUTOR: Fine.

CALLER: Thanks. Good-bye.

Now, it is time to dissect the dialogue. The caller opened with:

Hello, this is Martin Ericson calling from the Newtown Science Foundation. I am calling for Steven Pines.

Brevity is rewarded. What the caller should have said is:

Hello, this is Martin Erickson calling from the Newtown Science Foundation for Steven Pines.

A subtle point, but still worth making. His other mistakes are less subtle and more apt to cost him the potential contributor's support.

After the choppy introduction, the caller asked the potential contributor whether he could take a moment of his time. Never ask a potential contributor if you can take a moment of his time. All too often he will say no. Then you are stuck. The caller tried to recover by continuing with the call, even though the potential contributor let him know that it was not a good time. Not a bad recovery, but the problem could have been avoided had the caller simply told the potential contributor that he would take only a moment of his time and then continued on.

The caller then asked another question that never should have been asked. He inquired, "Have you supported us in the past?" The caller got exactly what he did not want: a negative response. What matters is not the potential contributor's giving history, but what he does this year.

Once again, the caller managed to recover. He began negotiating by asking for a $500 pledge. The problem here is how he presented the installment option. He said, ". . . And you can pay it in installments." What does that mean? Two installments of $250? Four installments of $125? Ten installments of $50? And how much time is to elapse between payment of each installment? Do not expect potential contributors to ask these questions. Be specific. The caller should have said, ". . . and you can pay this pledge in two installments of $250. The second installment would not be due for six months."

The potential contributor said no, so the caller rightfully asked for a more moderate amount. But what amount did he ask for? He said: "How about a pledge of $50 quarterly?" Did he mean $50 each quarter for a total pledge of $200? Or did he mean a $50 pledge to be paid in four installments of $12.50? He probably meant the former, not the latter. But did the potential contributor know this?

The caller followed the pledge request with another poorly phrased question: "Is that more reasonable?" A more appropriate question would be; "Is that amount more manageable for you?" This question does not undermine the caller's legitimacy by suggesting that his previous request was unreasonable.

Despite all the caller's mistakes, the potential contributor seemed vaguely interested. He asked for a form and some time to think about pledging. The job of the caller was to get a commitment that evening. The caller knew what his job was but not how to do it. He repeated the same unclear pledge request and then added: "Your commitment this evening will help us more than you know." Do not keep potential contributors in the dark. Tell them exactly how their commitment will help. The caller also missed the opportunity to clarify his ambiguous "$50" pledge request.

This phone call is full of problems from beginning to end. Perhaps its biggest problem was its end. The caller completely ignored the validation. This is especially disconcerting because (1) the amount of the pledge was unclear and (2) it is debatable whether there was a pledge at all.

Dialogue 2

CALLER: Hello, this is Lisa Lee calling from the Campolo for State Senator Campaign in St. Louis for Andrew Kraft.

INDIRECT CONTACT: This is Mrs. Kraft. How may I help you?

CALLER: If at all possible, I would like to speak with Mr. Kraft. He's expecting my call.

INDIRECT CONTACT: What do you want to speak with him about?

CALLER: I'd like to speak with him about the Campolo campaign.

INDIRECT CONTACT: Are you calling for money?

CALLER: Yes, among other things.

INDIRECT CONTACT: Well, we're busy.

CALLER: I realize you're very busy. I promise this will only take a moment. This probably will be the only opportunity that I will have to speak with him.

INDIRECT CONTACT: Hold one moment.

POTENTIAL CONTRIBUTOR: Hello, this is Mr. Kraft. What can I do for you?

CALLER: This is Lisa Lee calling from Campolo Headquarters in St. Louis. I'd like to talk with you for a few minutes about the State Senator's reelection efforts. We are facing stiff competition from our opponents. The Republicans have made Jeff Campolo one of their prime targets for defeat this November because of his liberal voting record on social issues—issues like abortion, prayer in the schools, and equal rights—issues that I am sure are as important to you as they are to Jeff.

The Republican state party is spending $50,000 to defeat him. We need money to fight back. That's why we are calling people like you for support.

We need to raise $20,000 by October 15 to ensure that we will have enough money to counteract the Republicans' effort to defeat us. We are hoping that you could help us reach the goal with a pledge of $300. How does that sound?

POTENTIAL CONTRIBUTOR: I'm sorry. I don't have that kind of money. I'm a retired union man. I'm not one of your fat cats. That's probably why I'm a Democrat.

CALLER: Well, we have more moderate levels of giving. Do you think you could support us in a more moderate way?

POTENTIAL CONTRIBUTOR: I'd really like to. But I don't have any money to spare.

CALLER: I understand. Well, whatever you give will be appreciated. Do you think you could give us a small gift as a token of your support? We really need your help.

POTENTIAL CONTRIBUTOR: Let me talk to my wife. Call me tomorrow.

CALLER: Do you think you could ask her now? We really would appreciate a commitment this evening.

POTENTIAL CONTRIBUTOR: Okay. (Pause) We can give $10.

CALLER: We were hoping for a minimum gift of $25. Do you think that you could manage that?

POTENTIAL CONTRIBUTOR: If $10 is not enough, you don't have to take anything.

CALLER: I'm sorry. We're very grateful for your pledge of $10.

POTENTIAL CONTRIBUTOR: Okay.

CALLER: Let me just confirm this. The amount of your pledge is $10. Your address is 1313 Mockingbird Lane, Adamsville, 60606?

POTENTIAL CONTRIBUTOR: Correct.

CALLER: I'll send you a pledge validation tomorrow as well as a postage-paid return envelope. It's been a real pleasure speaking with you. And thanks again.

The caller did an excellent job initially. She politely but persuasively convinced the potential contributor's spouse to put the potential contributor on the phone. She also concisely presented the potential contributor with strong reasons for him to support the campaign.

The problems began with the negotiations. The caller asked for $300. The potential contributor declined, replying that he was not a wealthy man. The caller then asked for a more moderate amount, but did not state what a more moderate amount might be. What is a more moderate amount? $275? $100? $5? The potential contributor could not have known what the caller meant. Not surprisingly, he declined again.

Once again, the caller pleaded for support. She asked for a small gift. But what is a small gift? Small in comparison to an undefined moderate amount?

Not only did the caller make a mistake by not asking for a specific dollar amount, she also make a mistake by referring to the gift as a "token." The term "token" belittles a gift. It is important that a potential contributor feels good about his gift, whatever the amount may be. Avoid words like "token," which have a contrary effect.

Well, a small gift sounded fine to Mr. Kraft, but he wanted to talk to his wife first. He asked to be called back the next day. The caller handled this one well, convincing Mr. Kraft to speak with his wife while she waited.

Mr. Kraft then told the caller he could give $10. This was the first dollar amount mentioned since the initial $300 request. Because the caller did not guide the negotiation process by requesting specific dollar amounts, the potential contributor decided what amount he thought was appropriate. At that point, all was lost for the caller. Because he relinquished control of the conversation, his attempt to regain control was seen as offensive by the potential contributor.

For all the time and money the caller invested in the call, she ended up with only $10. Is there any way she could have mitigated her losses? Of course. As with all calls, she should have asked the potential contributor whether he knew anyone else she could call. Equally important, this is a political campaign. There is always work to be done in a political campaign. The caller should have asked whether the potential contributor would be interested in lending a hand.

Dialogue 3

CALLER: Hello, this is Sally Evans calling from the Center City Ballet Company for Mr. Ronald Weisman.

POTENTIAL CONTRIBUTOR: This is he. What can I do for you?

CALLER: I'd like to speak with you for a moment about the ballet. As you may know, 70% of our support comes from people like you, people who appreciate what we have done and who want us to keep on doing it. We recently moved from 3rd Street to a spacious new home on 18th and Landers. We are trying to raise $3000 over the next three weeks to offset the costs of this move. The alternative is to cut out the free summer dance program for children. We are hoping that you could help us with a pledge of $300. Is this manageable?

POTENTIAL CONTRIBUTOR: Well, I support what you are doing. I saw your show last month and really enjoyed it. But right now I can't afford to make that kind of contribution. It's too high for me. I gave $50 last year, and I thought that was a lot.

CALLER: I appreciate your situation. How about a pledge of $75? That's only $25 more than last year's gift. And it works out to less than $2 a week.

POTENTIAL CONTRIBUTOR: I wish I could. I just don't have any money at the moment. I'm sorry. Why don't you call me next month? My financial situation should have improved by then. At least, I hope so.

CALLER: Okay, I'll try you then.

POTENTIAL CONTRIBUTOR: Thank you. You're very understanding.

The caller received a compliment from the potential contributor but nothing more. Where did she go wrong?

She lost control of the conversation when the potential contributor disclosed his giving history. The caller was correct to respond to the potential contributor's mention of his previous gift. It is always appropriate to respond to information furnished by the potential contributor. What was objectionable was how she responded. She dropped from a $300 request to a $75 request. She assumed that a potential contributor who gave $50 last year would be unlikely to give substantially more this year. That is an assumption she should not have made. Assume everyone can give and that everyone can give big. To avoid surrendering negotiating room, she should have said:

> We appreciate your previous support. We also are very happy that you continue to enjoy the ballet. We need an extra-special commitment this year. Do you think you could give us $50 now, and then again two more times throughout the year? That would be a total pledge of $150. Four months would separate the installments.

Even though the caller inappropriately dropped to $75, the potential contributor still was unable to pledge. He asked her to call him back next month. She followed his lead and as a consequence ended up with nothing. She should have stressed the importance of making a commitment that evening.

Script Writing

Now is the time to put everything together in a script. A sample script follows. Use this as a model for your own script. After the script, we will analyze each component.

The Script for the St. Ann Day Care Center

Introduction

Hello, this is (caller's name) calling from the St. Ann Day Care Center for (potential contributor's name).

(Potential contributor's name), I'd like to talk to you for a few minutes about the St. Ann Day Care Center. As you may know, this year the Day Care Center provided recreational activities for 200 children who otherwise would have had no supervised summer fun. Next year we want to offer our services to 300 children. We can do this only with community support. You see, grants from businesses and from the government account for only 30% of our budget. Seventy percent must come from people in the community like you. As I'm sure you realize, our whole community benefits when local children are occupied with worthwhile activities during their spare time.

Negotiations

That's why we hope that you can help us with a pledge of $500. Naturally, this gift will be tax-deductible. And you could pay it in two semiannual installments of $250. How does that sound (potential contributor's name)?

(If yes, validate.)
(If no, continue on down.)

Let's try something more moderate, a pledge of $300. That's actually less than $6 a week, and of course this gift also will be tax-deductible. To make it easier for you, I'll break it into two semiannual installments of $150. Can you manage a pledge of $300?

(If yes, validate.)
(If no, continue on down.)

Well, we have other meaningful levels of giving that are more affordable. And it's vital that we find one that's suitable for you. We're asking you to make the Day Care Center one of your top giving priorities this year. Without strong community support, we can't continue to grow. I hope you'll help us with a pledge of $200. This pledge is actually only 60¢ a day. We think the Center is worth that, and we hope you do, too. I'll even divide this pledge into four quarterly installments of $50. That means you will pay $50 now and then again three more times during the year. How about this (potential contributor's name)?

(If yes, validate.)
(If no, continue on down. Use chart on page 42.)

Validation

Thank you very much for your generous pledge of $_____ to be paid as soon as possible/semiannually/quarterly. Let's see, you're still at _____? (Confirm address.) I want you to know how much I appreciate this commitment. We need your payment/initial payment as soon as possible so we can plan next summer's program. Please send it in within two weeks.

By the way, do you or your husband/wife work for a matching gift company? (Ask the potential contributor to check this out on her own.)

You know, it's wonderful to find people like you who understand and care about us. We need more people like you. I have one more request. I hope you can give me the names and phone numbers of friends who share your concern. If you prefer, I won't mention your name when I call them.

I'll send you a pledge validation tomorrow as well as a postage-paid return envelope. Please include the validation with your check. That simplifies our record keeping. It's been a real pleasure speaking with you. Don't hesitate to call if you have any ideas to share with us. Once again (potential contributor's name), thank you for your pledge of $_____.

Analysis

The introduction and validation of each call are relatively standard. So are the first two or three pledge requests. Because they are standard, the script can clearly dictate how they should be approached.

The heart of the negotiation process is not standard. It will differ with each call so the script cannot be as specific here as it is with respect to the introduction, the initial requests, and the validation. An attempt to be exact in this area would produce an unworkable script.

While the script cannot dictate what the caller should say during the heart of negotiations, it can provide general guidelines. The negotiations chart is the mechanism that will accomplish this end. The chart provides the caller with a framework within which to proceed. Of course, when preparing your own script, you will make sure that the chart is not separate from the script, but part of it.

Column 1 gives the amount of the request; Column 2 gives the installment option that corresponds with each request; Column 3 breaks down the pledges, giving comparisons; and Column 4 provides additional information. It is in this column where information about the organization will go. In this particular script, timing is stressed. This organization decided that the cost of premiums and clubs outweighed their usefulness. If your organization decides to use them, you would describe them in additional columns, indicating clearly which premiums and/or clubs correspond to each level of giving.

While we speak in terms of vertical columns, it should be clear that the chart is used in horizontal rows. For example, if a caller asked a potential contributor for $150, he also might point out that as an option the potential contributor could pay his pledge in semiannual installments of $75 each; that the pledge actually is less than $3 per week; and that the day care center needs his money now, relating the information about the low-interest loan. Of course, callers will not always mention

Negotiating Chart

Ask for	Make it manageable	Break it down	Additional information
$150 Pledge	$75 Semiannually or $37.50 quarterly	Less than $3 a week Less than 50¢ a day (less than the cost of a cup of coffee)	We are in the process of negotiating a low-interest-rate bank loan. We can get this loan only if we show the bank that we have sufficient collateral. So you see, we need your help now so we can increase the services we offer. If we can't expand now, we might never have as good a chance.
$100 Pledge	$50 Semiannually or $25 quarterly	Less than $2 a week Less than 30¢ a day (less than the cost of the daily paper)	
$75 Pledge	$37.50 Semiannually	Less than $1.50 a week Less than 25¢ a day (the cost of a phone call)	Three day care centers in our area closed last year because they didn't have the funds to stay open. Your commitment this evening not only will help insure our survival, but it also will help us grow.
$50 Pledge	$25 Semiannually	Less than $1 a week Less than 15¢ a day	
$35 Pledge		Less than 70¢ a week Less than 10¢ a day	
$25 Pledge		Less than 50¢ a week Less than 8¢ a day	

each of these things at every level of giving. That would become tediously repetitive.

The Benefits of the Chart

The chart gives callers flexibility in deciding how much money to ask for next. For example, let's say that the caller asks a potential contributor for $200 and the potential contributor answers no. Normally, the next request would be for $150. But if the potential contributor sounded outraged, the next request would be for $100, instead.

The chart also gives callers the opportunity to use different phraseology with each request. For example, a request for $150 could be phrased this way: "How about a pledge of $150? You could pay that in two semiannual installments of $75. This pledge amounts to less than $3 a week." Compare this with a subsequent request for $100: "How about a pledge of less than 30¢ a day, less than the cost of the daily paper? That would be a pledge of $100. And, to make it convenient, you can pay $50 now and $50 in six months."

The chart provides two installment options, in many cases. For example, a $150 pledge can be paid in two installments of $75 or in four installments of $37.50. When a caller speaks with a potential contributor, however, he is to mention only one of the options. Specificity is rewarded.

The following dialogue shows you how to use the script you just read. Notice that the caller adds information to it to fit the occasion

CALLER: Hello, this is Mark Fels calling from the St. Ann Day Care Center for Marcella Washington.

POTENTIAL CONTRIBUTOR: This is Marcella.

CALLER: Marcella, I'd like to talk with you for a few minutes about the St. Ann Day Care Center. As you may know, this year the Center provided recreational activities for 200 children who otherwise would have had no supervised summer fun. Next year we want to offer our services to 300 children. We can do this only with community support. You see, grants from businesses and from the government account for only 30% of our budget. Seventy percent must come from people in the community like you. As I'm sure you realize, our whole community benefits when local children are occupied with worthwhile activities during their spare time. That's why we hope that you can help us with a pledge of $500. Naturally, this gift will be tax-deductible. And you could pay it in semiannual installments of $250. How does that sound, Marcella?

POTENTIAL CONTRIBUTOR: You've got to be kidding.

CALLER: Let's try something more moderate—a pledge of $300. That's actually less than $6 a week. And, of course, this gift also will be tax-deductible. To make it easier for you, I'll break it into two semiannual installments of $150. Can you manage a pledge of $300, Marcella?

POTENTIAL CONTRIBUTOR: You're still way too high.

CALLER: Well, we have other levels of giving that are more affordable. And it's vital that we find one that's suitable for you. We're asking you to make the Day Care Center one of your top giving priorities this year. Without strong community support, we can't continue to grow. I hope you'll help us with a pledge of $200. This pledge is actually only 60¢ a day. We think the Center is worth that; and we hope you do, too. I'll even divide this pledge into four quarterly installments of $50. That means you will pay $50 now and then again three more times during the year. How about this Marcella?

POTENTIAL CONTRIBUTOR: I don't want to waste your time. Let me make it easier for you. I'll pledge $25. I approve of what the Center is doing, but $25 is the best I can do.

CALLER: We appreciate your offer of support. But this year we need an extra-special commitment. We are in the process of negotiating a low-interest-rate bank loan. We can only get this loan if we show the bank that we have sufficient collateral. So you see, we need your help now so we can increase the services we offer. If we don't expand now, we might never have as good a chance. That's why I hope you can give us that $25 now and then three more times throughout the year for a total of $100. This pledge works out to only about 30¢ a day. That's less than the cost of the daily paper. We both know the Day Care Center is worth that much. This level of giving has been the most popular in our community. Most people find it manageable. Can I put you down for a $100 pledge today?

POTENTIAL CONTRIBUTOR: I don't like to commit in advance.

CALLER: Quite frankly, neither do I. But for something as important as the Day Care Center I would make an exception, and I hope you will, too. Can I put you down for that $100, Marcella? Remember, you only have to pay $25 now, your original offer. We have this installment plan for people like you, people who care about us but who can't pay a large pledge in one lump sum. We really are counting on you. How about it?

POTENTIAL CONTRIBUTOR: I understand. I'll explain this to my husband, and we'll get back to you when we decide.

CALLER: We really need your commitment now. As you may know, three day care centers in our area closed last year because they didn't have the funds to stay open. Your commitment this evening not only will help insure our survival, but it also will help us grow. So how about a $100 pledge?

POTENTIAL CONTRIBUTOR: Well, all right.

CALLER: Good! Thank you very much for your generous pledge of $100 to be paid in four quarterly installments of $25. Let's see, you are still at 2310 N. 6th Street, 19025?

POTENTIAL CONTRIBUTOR: That's right.

CALLER: I want you to know how much I appreciate this commitment. We need your initial payment as soon as possible so we can plan next summer's program. Please send it in within two weeks. By the way, do you or your husband work for a matching gift company?

POTENTIAL CONTRIBUTOR: I'm not sure.

CALLER: Please check on this at work as soon as possible. You know, it is wonderful to find people like you who understand and care about us. We need more people like you. I have one more request. I hope you can give me the names and phone numbers of some friends who share your concern for the Center. If you prefer, I won't mention your name when I call them.

POTENTIAL CONTRIBUTOR: Well, let's see, I guess you can call Lynn Block. Her number is 545-1235. It's okay with me if you mention my name.

CALLER: That's great, Marcella. I'll send you a pledge validation tomorrow as well as a postage-paid return envelope. Please include the validation with your check. That simplifies our record keeping. It's been a real pleasure speaking with you. Don't hesitate to call if you have ideas to share with us. Once again, thank you for your pledge of $100.

There are a number of reasons why this dialogue resulted in a sizeable pledge, despite the objections the potential contributor threw at the negotiator. The conciseness of the dialogue is one of its strengths. Mark respected Marcella's time and did not interject fluff into the conversation. That is, he avoided meaningless statements and questions intended to ingratiate himself.

In only a few words, he told Marcella (1) *what the Day Care Center currently is doing to help the community* (". . . this year the Center provided recreational activities for 200 children who otherwise would have had no supervised summer fun"); (2) *what it plans to do* ("Next year we want to offer our services to 300 children"); (3) *where the funding comes from* ("Grants from businesses and from the government account for only 30% of our budget. Seventy percent must come from people in the community like you"); and (4) *how Marcella can help the Center and at the same time help herself* (". . . our whole community benefits when local children are occupied with worthwhile activities during their spare time"). Mark subtly emphasized the word "our" in this statement, so Marcella could make the link between her interests and the Center's.

So as not to dilute the impact of what he had just told her, Mark immediately began to negotiate and was not bashful about starting high or about progressing downward in gradual steps, despite Marcella's surprised rejection of his initial $500 request. He used installments and comparisons to make his further requests palatable.

Instead of being stymied by Marcella's small offer of $25, he intensified negotiations by stressing timing (". . . we need an extra-special commitment. We are in the process of negotiating a low-interest-rate bank loan. We can only get this loan if we show the bank that we have sufficient collateral. . . . If we can't expand now, we might never have as good a chance'').

Marcella is human. She doesn't like to make commitments about money. Instead of arguing, Mark agreed with her. But, to encourage her to give $100 in installments, he emphasized that he personally would make an exception for the Day Care Center. He no doubt pleased Marcella by implying that she is one of a fine group of citizens, people who care about the Center but who just cannot pay a large pledge in one lump sum.

Marcella then exhibited another very human trait, passing the buck ("I'll explain this to my husband, and we'll get back to you when we decide"). Mark, instead of being defeated, responded persuasively and hit hard on the fact that three day care centers in the area closed last year because of lack of funds.

Now that you have studied the script and learned how a productive dialogue flows from it, you can clearly see that the sample script itself is very basic. Accordingly, it is easy to adapt. To demonstrate how easy it is to adapt the basic script to your own organization, a second sample script follows. You will notice that the format and language are similar, despite the fact that the prior script involved a community day care center and the following script involves a political action group. In fact, there are only a few differences between the scripts, which we will discuss after you read them both.

Following the script is a sample dialogue based on the script. Here again you will notice many similarities. Just as the scripts are similar, so are the corresponding dialogues. Negotiating techniques do not vary between organizations. The truth is that if you can do telephone fund raising for one organization, you can do it for another.

The Script for the Coalition for Fair Taxation

Introduction

Hello, this is (caller's name) calling from the Coalition for Fair Taxation for (potential contributor's name).

(Potential contributor's name), I'd like to speak with you for a few minutes about the Coalition for Fair Taxation. As you may have heard from some of the other prominent business people in town, we are concerned that the business community might take the brunt of the proposed increase in state taxes. We don't want to waste any time before letting our state legislators know about our concern. We are doubling our lobbying efforts, and that is why we need your support immediately. Next month may be too late. Irrevocable decisions may have been made by then.

Negotiations

That's why we hope that you can help us with a pledge of $500 this evening. Normally, we would offer you the option of paying this pledge in installments. Unfortunately, because of the urgency of our need, installment payments are not practical. But you could put your pledge on your credit card and arrange the payments to suit yourself. And as our way of saying thank you for your generous support, we will send you a tie/scarf, imprinted with the Coalition emblem as well as a bi-monthly newsletter to keep you up-to-date on the success of our lobbying efforts. How does that sound?

(If yes, validate.)
(If no, continue on down.)

Let's try something more moderate, a pledge of $300. That's actually less than $6 a week. As our way of saying thank you, we will send you a lapel pin embossed with the organization's emblem and of course the newsletter. Can you manage a pledge of $300?

(If yes, validate.)
(If no, continue on down.)

Well, we have other levels of giving that are more affordable. And its vital that we find one that's suitable for you. We're asking you to make the Coalition one of your top giving priorities this year. Without strong support from the business community, we will not be able to defeat the proposed tax increase. I hope you'll help us with a pledge of $200. This pledge actually is less than $4 a week, less than 60¢ a day. Once again, let me remind you, you can put this pledge on your credit card and pay it at your convenience. How about it (potential contributor's name)? (At this level of giving, the potential contributor will also receive the lapel pin, as well as the newsletter.)

(If yes, validate.)
(If no, continue on down. Use the chart on page 48.)

Validation

Thank you very much for your generous pledge of $_____. Let's see, you're still at (confirm address)? I want you to know how much I appreciate this commitment. We need your payment as soon as possible. Please send us it within one week.

Negotiating Chart

Ask for	Break it down	Premiums	Additional information
$150 Pledge	Less than $3 a week Less than 50¢ a day (less than the cost of a cup of coffee)		Last year, a similar bill passed in Chester County. We can see for ourselves how the business community there has been hurt by it. They're trying to undo the harm that has already been done. We're trying to prevent the harm from ever occurring. And believe me, it's much easier to defeat a bill than it is to repeal it.
$100 Pledge	Less than $2 a week Less than 30¢ a day (less than the cost of the daily paper)	Two coalition coffee mugs	
$75 Pledge	Less than $1.50 a week Less than 25¢ a day (the cost of a phone call)		We are going to meet with our lobbyists soon to let them know what their budget will be. Your commitment this evening will help insure that we have the money we need to fight and to win.
$50 Pledge	Less than $1 a week Less than 15¢ a day	One coalition coffee mug	
$35 Pledge	Less than 70¢ a week Less than 10¢ a day	Coalition bumper sticker	
$25 Pledge	Less than 50¢ a week Less than 8¢ a day		

It is wonderful to find people like you who appreciate what we're doing. We need more people like you. I have one more request. I hope you can give me the names and phone numbers of friends who share your concern. If you prefer, I won't mention your name when I call.

I'll send you a pledge validation tomorrow as well as a postage-paid return envelope. Please include the validation with your check. That simplifies our record keeping. It's been a real pleasure speaking with you. Don't hesitate to call if you have ideas to share with us. Once again, (potential contributor's name), thank you for your pledge of $_____.

As you see, the sample scripts are very similar. The dissimilarities reflect the differences between the organizations, not a difference in negotiating techniques.

The dissimilarities are as follows: first, the Coalition uses premiums, and the script reflects this. Second, the Coalition does not offer the installment option. This is because the Coalition needs money immediately and cannot afford to allow potential contributors to defer payments. It is because the Coalition cannot afford to offer the installment option that it decided to use premiums and to pursue the credit card option vigorously. Third, the Coalition did not mention matching gift companies in the pledge validation. This is because few companies, if any, match gifts to political organizations. Fourth, the due date of Coalition pledges is one week after the pledge is made, not two, because of the immediate need. Finally, the facts about the organizations differ because the organizations themselves differ. Although the particular facts differ, both scripts use them in precisely the same way: to convince potential contributors to give now and to give big.

A sample dialogue follows based on the Coalition script.

CALLER: Hello, this is Beth Le Compte calling from the Coalition for Fair Taxation for Jason Roberts.

POTENTIAL CONTRIBUTOR: Beth, you've caught me on a bad day.

CALLER: I'm sorry I called at a busy time. I assure you that this will take only a few minutes.

POTENTIAL CONTRIBUTOR: I suppose I might as well give you five minutes. But that's all I can spare.

CALLER: Jason, as you may have heard from some of the other prominent business people in town, we are concerned that the business community might take the brunt of the proposed increase in state taxes. We don't want to waste any time before letting our state legislators know about our concern. We are doubling our lobbying efforts, and that is why we need your support immediately. Next month may be too late. Irrevocable decisions may have been made by then.

POTENTIAL CONTRIBUTOR: How much are you asking for?

CALLER: People around town, realizing the gravity of this, have been generous. A $500 pledge from you will go a long way toward making sure our views are heard by the right ears. Normally we would offer you the option of paying this pledge in installments. Unfortunately, because of the urgency of our need, installments payments are not practical. But you could put your pledge on your credit card and arrange the payments to suit yourself. And, as our way of saying thank you, we will send you a tie imprinted with the coalition emblem as well as a bi-monthly newsletter to keep you up-to-date on the success of our lobbying efforts. How does that sound, Jason?

POTENTIAL CONTRIBUTOR: $500! That's a heck of a lot of money. How much are others giving?

CALLER: Most of the others are giving as much as they can possibly afford. They know that if we just sit back and keep quiet, we'll lose our shirts. In fact, last year a similar bill passed in Chester County. We can see for ourselves how the business community there has been hurt by it. They're trying to undo the harm that has already been done. We're trying to prevent the harm from ever occurring. And, believe me, Jason, it's much easier to defeat a bill than it is to repeal it.

POTENTIAL CONTRIBUTOR: Well, look, I can't come up with $500, not even if I use my credit card.

CALLER: Let's try something more moderate, then—a pledge of $300. That's actually less than $6 a week. As our way of saying thank you, we will send you a lapel pin embossed with the organization's emblem and of course the newsletter. Can you manage a pledge of $300?

POTENTIAL CONTRIBUTOR: I wish this had come up earlier. I budgeted my big contribution this year for Citizens for Efficient Local Government. I can't let them down.

CALLER: That's a good organization. But a major effort now by the Coalition for Fair Taxation will help your business thrive so that you can support local groups like that generously in the future. A severe tax increase will do the opposite. We have other levels of giving that are more affordable. And it's vital that we find one that's suitable for you. We're asking you to make the Coalition one of your top giving priorities this year. Without strong support from the business community, we will not be able to defeat the proposed tax increase. I hope you'll help us with a pledge of $200. This pledge is less than $4 a week; in fact, it's less than 60¢ a day. How about this, Jason? Let me remind you once again that you could put your pledge on your credit card and pay it at your convenience.

POTENTIAL CONTRIBUTOR: Well, I suppose I could think about it and let you know next week.

CALLER: Jason, it's good of you to suggest that. But I really must know where we stand, so we can notify our lobbyists. We are meeting with them on Friday afternoon to let them know what their budget will be. Your commitment this evening will help insure that we have the money we need to fight and to win. How about a pledge of $150 this evening?

POTENTIAL CONTRIBUTOR: All right. I'll do it!

CALLER: Thank you very much for your generous pledge of $150. Let's see, your address is still 619 Marshall Road, Belmont, 93023?

POTENTIAL CONTRIBUTOR: That's correct.

CALLER: I want you to know, Jason, how much I appreciate this commitment. Because of the urgency of the situation, we need your payment as soon as possible. Please send it to us within one week.

You know, it's wonderful to find people like you who appreciate what we are doing. We need more people like you. I have one more request. I hope you can give me the names and phone numbers of friends who share your concern about fair taxation. If you prefer, I won't mention your name when I call.

POTENTIAL CONTRIBUTOR: Call Joe Rohrlich. He's mad as hell about the proposed tax increase. I don't have his number handy, but you can call him at the office during the day. He's the president of Rohrlich Electronics. And tell him Jason sent you.

CALLER: I'll call him this afternoon. Thanks! I'll send you a pledge validation tomorrow as well as a postage-paid return envelope. Please include the validation with your check. That simplifies our record keeping. It's been a real pleasure talking with you, Jason. Don't hesitate to call if you have ideas to share with us. Once again, thank you for your pledge of $150.

Even though the potential contributor tried to postpone the conversation, the caller persuaded him to hear her out then and there. This is usually best. Most potential contributors will admit that there is really no convenient time for them to talk with you. Everyone has to make time.

To make sure she had his attention, Beth immediately did two things. She referred to his peers ("As you may have heard from some of the other prominent business people in town . . .") and appealed to his self-interest (". . . the business community might take the brunt of the proposed tax increase").

She took only 20 seconds to tell him how the Coalition will respond to the crisis ("We don't want to waste any time before letting our state legislators know about our concern. We are doubling our lobbying efforts . . .") and intensified the impact of what she has to say by stressing timing ("Next month might be too late. Irrevocable decisions may have been made by then").

Beth responded to Jason's questions about how much money the Coalition needs from him by again referring to his peers ("People around town, realizing the gravity of this, have been generous") and again appealing to his self-interest ("A $500 pledge from you will go a long way toward making sure our views are heard by the right ears"). With the little word "our," she let Jason know that his well-being and the activities of the Coalition are compatible. She repeated this pattern of emphasizing what Jason's peers are doing, followed by an appeal to his self-interest ("Most of the others are giving as much as they can possibly afford. They know that if we just sit back and keep quiet, we'll lose our shirts").

When Jason tried to beg off because he already had budgeted a contribution to another group, Beth coolly praised the rival group and suggested that a pledge to the Coalition now would insure that he has the funds to contribute handsomely to the other group later.

Beth brought the negotiations to a successful conclusion by sliding past Jason's final attempt to put her off ("I suppose I could think about it and let you know next week"). She countered by stressing urgency and ultimate victory ("Your commitment this evening will help insure that we have the money to fight and to win"). Note that throughout the dialogue Beth did not pander to Jason but spoke to him as one business person to another.

2

DEVELOPING A COTERIE OF
TOP-NOTCH CALLERS

Paid Callers or Volunteers: Which Is Right
for You?

Developing a coterie of good callers is all important. With good callers, your program will flourish. Without them, it will flounder. You first must decide whether to use paid callers or volunteers. To make this decision, you must weigh the advantages and disadvantages of using volunteers.

The Advantages of Using Volunteers as Callers

1. Using volunteers obviously saves money.
2. Volunteer callers are genuinely enthusiastic about the cause and therefore are eager to become good callers.
3. Some potential contributors are more generous when called by volunteers. It seems to take the commercial onus off the call and turn it into something resembling a neighbor-to-neighbor discussion.

The Disadvantages of Using Volunteers as Callers

1. Expect a high turnover rate. Volunteers may be there because of momentary lulls in their lives—a hiatus between jobs, time on their hands while their children are in school, and so on. When their situation changes, it's often farewell to you.
2. Volunteers have home, school, and career responsibilities. You will come second, behind these responsibilities, if there is a clash.
3. Some volunteers may not work diligently; they may be supersen-

sitive, even childish; they may get huffy at criticism. They may believe that since they are not being paid, they should be their own boss.

Callers must show up when scheduled. They must work diligently. They must accept constructive criticism, not with tears or anger but with gratitude, because how else will they improve? The point is that using volunteer callers makes the payroll look good, but it may cost you thousands of dollars if potential contributors are turned off by bungling callers who are not held to the same high standards as paid callers.

4. But the biggest problem with volunteers is finding them. Although some prestigious organizations (big-city art museums, for example) actually have waiting lists of would-be volunteers, in general volunteers are becoming harder to find. Many women, who in past years would have been ardent volunteers, are holding down full-time jobs. Because of this shortage of volunteers, you will have to work hard to attract good ones, and once they are under your wing, you will have to treat them well so they will stay with you. This takes time, and time is money. The time you spend finding and keeping volunteers may negate your savings.

Usually the disadvantages of using volunteers outweigh the advantages. The adage "you get what you pay for" holds true in telephone fund raising. Therefore, we recommend as a general rule that you use paid callers. There are, however, three situations in which volunteers will be your best bet.

1. Political campaigns can almost always get away with using volunteers. In fact, political campaigns usually have more volunteers than they need. The excitement of a campaign attracts people. In addition, because campaigns are close-ended (that is, everyone knows when they will end), people are willing to make a commitment, knowing it will be short-term. During a campaign, emotions run high and produce energy, stamina, and the desire to participate. Therefore, political campaigns do not need to offer callers a financial incentive.

2. Organizations getting by on a shoestring will be eager to try telephone fund raising, but may be able to manage it only by using volunteers all the way through their program. In this case, the advantage of using volunteers is plain: without them, there would be no telephone fund raising at all.

3. One-shot deals also should use volunteers. Why? First, it would be difficult to find good callers who are willing to accept such short-term employment. Second, it should not be difficult to find volunteers. Because one-shot deals are close-ended, like political campaigns, people are willing to make a commitment. While nonpolitical one-shot deals

may not attract quite as many people as hard-fought political campaigns do, if you publicize the event early and start looking for callers soon after, you should have no trouble developing a coterie of volunteers.

The following sections tell you how to find, hire, train, coach, supervise, reward, and fire callers. Most of the principles discussed will apply with equal force whether you use volunteers or paid callers. Where there are differences, they will be explained.

Advertising

How to Word Your Advertisement

A clear, direct advertisement will insure that you get the type of callers you need—articulate and assertive. The advertisement is actually the first step in screening out applicants who cannot do the job, so do not be afraid to be blunt about your needs. For example: "We need articulate, assertive people to negotiate large commitments over the phone for the University Hospital. Interested? Call Kay at 555-1313 for a phone interview. Salary plus bonuses. A few evenings each week."

If you are using volunteers, there must be something in the advertisement to attract them to your cause. Volunteering is a two-way street. There must be something in it for the person offering the help as well as for the person receiving it. Consider these advertisements from just a single month's classifieds in a national publication:

. . . is looking for a few good interns. The work may not always fulfill your utmost creative potential and it won't pay anything, but it's a great way to become familiar with the workings of a magazine and will add éclat to your resume. Besides, we're fun to work with! We'd want a certain level of commitment in return for the training and exposure offered . . . .

. . . is looking for live-in volunteers for a village for mentally handicapped adults. House-parenting/work in garden, weavery, bakery or woodshop. Generous benefits. . . .

. . . is looking for 100 volunteers, some to travel worldwide. Action for environmental repair, total nuclear disarmament, new world economic order. . . .

Notice that each advertisement presents a lure: becoming familiar with how a magazine is put together, adding brilliance to a resume, having fun, receiving free housing and benefits, or traveling around the world. It is the familiar principle of self-interest, the same principle you emphasize with potential contributors. What is the incentive for your volunteers? Sit down and figure this out so you can present your best face to potential volunteers, who, in fact, are as important as potential contributors. Their gift of time is as valuable as a gift of money.

In addition to being worded so that it will entice volunteers, your advertisement must be worded so that only those who are qualified will answer. Volunteers, like paid callers, must be chosen selectively. In both cases, the advertisement is the first step in the selection process. Try something like this: "We need you plus a few other articulate, assertive volunteers to negotiate large commitments over the phone for the Snake River Restoration Fund. What will you get out of it? A beautiful, clean river to go boating on, swimming in, and fishing out of. In addition, we will teach you the techniques of negotiating. Think of it as taking a course—at no charge—in assertiveness training. If you're the person who can take on an important assignment like this, call Betty at 555-2121 between 9 AM and 1 PM."

Where to Advertise

1. The Sunday paper. Expect a large response. That will give you a great many people from which to select. But because advertising in a Sunday paper is expensive, do so only if you are looking for a large response.

2. Special interest newspapers. You will find them in the yellow pages. Be highly selective. Choose those papers that are read by the kind of people you want: bright, articulate, and assertive. But do not think that choosing a newspaper with an outstanding group of readers will relieve you of the burden of careful screening.

3. College and university newspapers. Colleges and universities are gold mines because students usually know how to talk and how to listen. Moreover, school newspapers often allow non-profit-making organizations to advertise at a discount.

4. Biweekly and monthly publications. They will bring in people steadily but in small numbers over a prolonged time span.

5. Radio. It may not cost as much as you imagine. It may even be free if your advertisement is presented as a public service announcement. There are currently no specific Federal Communiciations Commission requirements about airing public service announcements, but there is a general requirement that stations do programming that is in the public interest. Many stations look favorably on public service an-

nouncements, therefore. Airing them consistently makes the station look good when its license to broadcast comes up for renewal.

Look in the yellow pages of the telephone book to see which stations are best for you. Most have a specialty: day-long news, talk shows, programming in Spanish, country music, classical music, gospel music, soft rock, and so on. This makes it easy to target your message; that is, to get it across to the people you most want to reach.

When you contact the stations you select, let them know that you are a non-profit-making organization. Some stations, especially those connected with colleges and universities, will give you free air time. Others will charge but give a discount.

If you decide to buy air time, buy at least ten 30-second spots. Less than this number will not give you enough exposure to judge whether radio advertising produces the results you want. You can stack these spots up; that is, you can air them for several weeks at the single most-listened-to time (Saturday night, for example, if you choose a station specializing in romantic music). Or, you can air them often and daily. Or, you can combine these two approaches.

In addition to garnering callers, radio advertising also will give your organization good name exposure. Let's say you decide to advertise on a station specializing in "oldies" (music that was popular 30 to 40 years ago) because you think its retired listeners might be looking for part-time jobs. Your message also will be heard by a slightly younger age group with considerable disposable income because many are near the peak of their earning power. Your message, therefore, will be absorbed both by potential employees and potential contributors.

Alternatives to Advertising

1. The callers. The callers themselves will help you replenish the calling pool if you make it worth their while. Award them a $5 bonus for everyone they refer who is hired and stays at least a month. With the expectation of bonus money, callers will try to bring in friends and family. Do not assume family members or members of the same peer group will be uniformly good callers. Judge each applicant on his merits, not on his connections within the calling coterie.

2. Flyers. Have 1000 printed. It will not cost much more than having 500 or less printed. Brainstorm with your associates, and together think of as many places as possible to post the flyers. In addition, carry some with you wherever you go and post them in places where would-be callers might congregate. Callers go places you do not. Encourage them to carry a few flyers around with them to post in likely places.

Your flyers should look good—professionally printed. If you have a logo, use it. The flyer should give the same information as the advertisement you use in the paper. It, too, will screen out people who cannot do the job.

How Much Advertising Do You Need?

If you are doing political telephone fund raising, you probably will not need to advertise at all. You probably will have an influx of volunteers from which to select callers. If you do need to recruit callers, the best methods are flyers and word of mouth. Both are inexpensive and effective. Resort to newspaper or radio advertising only if the less expensive methods fall short.

If your program is a one-shot deal, start recruiting callers, using flyers and word of mouth, as soon as you decide to have the program. If you start early enough and vigorously enough, you might not have to advertise for callers at all. You can spend your money publicizing the event instead. That way, the community will be well aware of your organization and its needs when you call.

If your program is ongoing and your coterie of callers relatively large (15 or more), advertising will be a regular part of your program. Your calling coterie will probably be an eclectic group: students; people who are between jobs; actors, artists, and musicians supplementing meager incomes; women returning to work after years at home; retirees looking for something useful to do; and so on. Consequently, most callers will not have a long-term commitment to your program. As their situation changes, so will yours. It is entirely normal for the calling coterie to be in a dynamic state of flux with callers continually leaving and then being replaced by new callers.

Nonetheless, as your program settles down, chances are that you will find yourself with a nucleus of callers on whom you can rely. They like the work and know they are good at it and can make money at it. Do not become unduly complacent, though. Even this productive little group could vanish overnight. It is a great mistake to let the number of people in the calling coterie get down so low that in desperation you have to lower your hiring standards. It is better to augment at a steady pace to match your attrition rate.

Once you start to advertise in a number of sources, you will want to track the results, so you can spend your money where it does the most good. Every time you hire a caller, ask how she heard about the job. Keep an informal record of that information. If you discover that a source produces a large number of hireable applicants, continue to use it. Conversely, if a source is not productive, discontinue it.

Which Size Advertisement Should You Buy?

Start with the smallest you can buy. Usually, the inexpensive classifieds do as well or better than larger advertisements. Part-time job seekers are used to reading the classifieds. They look there first and may even skip over a more prominent advertisement.

Hiring

You have received an impressive response to your advertisements. Now you must determine which applicants to hire. Be very selective. More than anything else, the quality of your callers will determine the amount of money you raise.

The Telephone Interview

Your first contact with an aspiring caller will be by phone. This will not be the usual casual contact between a job seeker and an employer that does little more than set a time for an interview. This will be an interview itself. If the person is good on the phone, you will want to meet him in person, of course, but do not expect the in-person interview to be as revealing as the phone interview during which you have nothing to concentrate on but the applicant's telephone skills.

You can get an idea from the following list what sort of questions will tell you whether the applicant is capable of negotiating persuasively and raising money assertively:

1. What qualities do you have that make this telephone job a good one for you?
2. Are you good at thinking quickly? (Of course, if they cannot answer this, you have your answer.)
3. What other work do you do?
4. What subjects are you studying in school?
5. Why did you apply for this job?

Avoid questions that can be answered with a yes or no. It is perfectly okay to let an applicant know that you need to hear her talk. If you cannot get her to engage in a sensible conversation, this is a strong indication that she is not suited for the job.

Also, do not question applicants about their personal lives. Questions about their personal lives are not relevant and asking them is risky. You may hear information you do not want to hear. Let's say an applicant tells you she is a political activist. If she turns out to be unsuitable for the job, you may be accused of discriminating against her because of her activism.

If you discover that an applicant is unsuitable, save his time and yours by ending the interview quickly. Simply take his name and phone number, telling him you will call him if the need arises. Always thank him warmly for applying for the position.

The Personal Interview

Invite applicants who impress you on the phone to a personal interview. Be careful not to dominate the interview yourself. It is not your job at this point to tell the applicant the details of the job. Save that for the handful of superior people you hire. Right now your job is to get the applicant talking and keep her talking long enough for pronunciation peculiarities and the like to emerge. You do this by asking questions similar to those you asked during the phone interview which call for more than a yes or no answer.

It is also your job to help the applicant relax. Relax yourself, therefore. The more relaxed you are, the more relaxed she will be. The sooner the applicant relaxes, the sooner she will begin to talk naturally. You can size her up more realistically after she stops her formal "interview" behavior and becomes herself.

Negotiating large pledges requires imagination and style, just the qualities that turn up in people who sometimes appear eccentric. Never reject anyone simply because he does not look or think exactly like everyone else. On the other hand, keep an eye open for troublesome quirks that might disrupt the calling session. For example, if someone has an excessively loud voice, he will destroy the concentration of the callers near him and, therefore, no matter how good he is, will not be an asset in the calling coterie.

Do not make the mistake of trying to save time by interviewing people in groups. Believe it or not, a first-rate university tried this when they were in a hurry to get their program started. Among the questions asked the group members was, "Do you think you can do this job?" Of course, they all answered yes. They all were hired, and most of them had to be let go—after their ineffective calls wasted valuable potential contributors. This illustrates another point: not all smart people make good callers. Certainly it takes brains, but it also takes assertiveness and tact.

Be careful of your own biases. Let's say you are a feminist and think displaced housewives would find calling appealing as a reentry into the working world. Fine, but do not give them the benefit of the doubt during the interview. Put them through the same tests as anyone else. In the long run, you will be doing them a favor by insisting they measure up to the same standards.

If in doubt about hiring someone, have him call you from one of the calling room phones and ask you for money for the cause. Let him study the script for a few minutes. He will be jittery. This procedure is not what he expected and he will be under stress, so you will have to allow for dozens of mistakes. But you will be able to assess how quickly he thinks. Chances are that someone who can think quickly, especially under stress, will be a super caller.

If a substantial number of the applicants who you interview in person are unsuitable, this means you are not screening carefully enough over the phone. Start screening more rigorously.

Those applicants who impress you favorably at the personal interview should be hired immediately. At that point, tell them more about the job and invite them to the next training session. As we discuss later, every caller must attend a training session before he begins calling.

If you use volunteers, hold them to the same standards you would paid callers. Do not feel that you cannot afford to be as selective when you recruit volunteers as you would be if you were hiring callers. If your organization is short of funds, how can you afford not to be selective? Steer inarticulate or unassertive volunteers to the clerical part of your program. Remember, once volunteers are part of the calling coterie, they will have to produce or be let go. Which is more humiliating, not being hired or being let go after a bungled effort? Obviously, the latter. Taking on someone inept out of misplaced kindness only delays the day of reckoning.

A problem may arise if your organization has been nurturing a loyal group of volunteers who want to try their hand at calling now that your organization has a telephone fund-raising program. You do not want to anger them, of course. Nevertheless, do not let anyone into the calling coterie, no matter how eager she is to try it, unless she is also bright, articulate, and assertive.

How Many Callers Is Too Many?

Many a night worried directors lie awake, wondering where in the world they are going to put those new people, every one of them too good not to hire. After all, there are only so many phones. But almost never does the number of phones exceed the number of callers, no matter how many new ones are hired. Keep in mind that you have two elimination processes yet to go through after hiring. Some of those hired will not show up for training, and some of those who show up for training will not show up to call. Often, luckily for you, it will be the very people you were in doubt about. They, too, were unsure so they eliminated themselves. If you do find yourself with more callers than phones, simply ask a few of your less productive callers to take the night off with pay. If these callers are volunteers, your heartfelt thanks will have to do.

Training

Everyone—volunteer as well as paid caller—must be trained before beginning to call. You have carefully selected a number of people who you believe have promise, but they need to be trained before their promise can be realized.

Some would-be callers, usually those with sales experience, may insist that they do not need to be trained. No prior sales or fund-raising experience can substitute for training. No matter how extensive the would-be caller's prior experience, he will benefit from training. In addition to learning the relevant facts about your organization, he will learn ingenious negotiating techniques that no doubt will be new to him. He even may have to unlearn bad habits, and the training session is the best place to do this.

How to Coordinate Hiring with Training

Schedule a training for the very next weekend after your advertisement runs. That way when good people come in, you can get them into the calling coterie right away.

It is important not to crowd too many people into one training. Split it up—20 people is maximum—perhaps by scheduling trainings on different days, a Saturday and a Sunday, for example, or by letting a trusted assistant handle the overflow.

Occasionally, people who drift in when you do not have a training coming up will try to convince you that they do not need training. For the reasons given earlier, do not believe them. Do not let these people get away, either. When you run across a gem, hire him. It is okay to hold a training for as few as two or three people.

You might be strongly tempted to abbreviate training when you expect only a few people at the session. Don't. If there is just a handful of new callers, training will shorten itself naturally. It is dangerous for the program as well as unfair to new callers to deliberately shorten training. A semiprepared caller will take longer to become productive on the phone. In other words, an abbreviated training leads only to longer on-the-job training, which wastes potential contributors.

What should you do if you expect less than two or three people at a training? You do not want a one-on-one encounter. On the other hand, if you do not get these would-be callers into the calling coterie immediately, they might look for other work. The solution is to invite callers who already are in the calling coterie to join the session for retraining. In fact, if a good caller grows stale and is having a prolonged unproductive spell, retrain him without hesitation. (After all, he will be paid for it at his normal hourly wage.) Good callers are hardly expendable. Retraining a stale caller is far easier than hiring and training a new one. A few callers may balk at retraining and consider it an indignity, but others may be insulted if they are not included. Do not hesitate to invite even those callers who are doing well, if you think they will benefit. Superior callers sometimes begin to style their negotiations to suit themselves and, while they may be productive, they may not be as productive as they could be. They sometimes go too far astray and need to be reminded of the basic techniques of sound negotiating.

When and Where to Hold the Training

Learning how to do telephone fund raising will encompass a whole day: five to six hours with a break for lunch. Because most callers will have full-time jobs, Saturday and Sunday are the only practical days on which to schedule training.

Will would-be callers attend an all-day training? Yes! They will be getting paid for it. (But they should be paid only after one month of productive calling. This way you will not be rewarding people who attend training as a free lesson in how to raise funds for their favorite organization, not yours.)

Will volunteers attend an all-day training? Here, again, the answer is yes! You probably will have far less trouble persuading volunteers to attend then you might anticipate, for these reasons:

1. Training reinforces the idea of selectivity. Yours is a demanding organization, and you obviously expect these volunteers, selected as the brightest, most articulate, and most assertive, to do well.
2. Training gives volunteer callers confidence which they can get no other way. They will be smart enough to realize this.

3. Training makes their volunteer experience more valuable as resume material.
4. Training to work as a volunteer has a long tradition behind it.
   Board members are accustomed to going on daylong or even
   weekend-long board retreats. Volunteers with national organizations—fraternal groups, for example—very often attend conven-
   tions where they are expected to fill up a whole week with work-
   shops and the like.

If volunteers tell you they cannot take time to attend the training,
they may renege when you expect them to show up to call. Not much is
lost, therefore, if these people drop out when they realize training is
mandatory.

Extremely short one-shot deals as well as political campaigns close
to election day probably will have to do without an all-day training. If
your callers only will be calling for two or three days, for example, it may
be tough to get them to attend an all-day training. The ratio of training
time to work time is just too high. Likewise, if you are in the middle of a
highly charged and most likely severely disorganized political campaign, you will not have time to conduct structured, daylong trainings.
Instead, in both cases give truncated trainings, which are discussed later
in this section. Read this entire section even if you will be giving only
truncated trainings, because a truncated training is based on a full-scale
training.

The training room does not need to be cavernous. The more inti-
mate the better, in fact, because what the director has to say automatical-
ly becomes more conversational that way.

Good ventilation is important, too. Remember, callers will be
spending almost an entire day in one room. You do not want them to
doze off because the room is stuffy.

Finally, the seating arrangement is important. Do not arrange your
room like a classroom where some can sit in the back and let their minds
wander. A circle is best, both most efficient and most pleasant. The new
callers will relax and participate, insuring a productive give-and-take.

Training Style

Enthusiasm is contagious, as we have said. Potential contributors
pick it up from callers, and callers pick it up from the director. Therefore,
the director must convey her enthusiasm in no uncertain terms.

Not only must the director be enthusiastic, but she also must be friendly. Training is a colleague-to-colleague learning experience. If the director is too authoritarian, people will not absorb easily what she says.

What to Do in the Morning

After giving your new callers an exuberant welcome, the first thing you need to do is instill them with confidence. Telephone fund raising is not easy. The sooner your callers begin to develop the self-confidence needed to do it right, the better. Instill confidence by letting them know how special they are. Explain the process by which they were chosen. Tell them how many applied and how few were selected. Let them know that you have faith in their calling ability and that otherwise they would not be there.

Next, explain the overall goal of training: to prepare would-be callers to do telephone fund raising well. Let them know that over the next few hours they will receive a great deal of information, too much to absorb completely in one day. Explain that they need not master everything during training and that when calling begins everything they learn at training will fall into place. These are the same words of encouragement we gave you earlier in the book.

After this brief introduction, it is time to tell them about your organization. Only tell them what you think they can remember. Among these facts should be your organization's purpose, goals, history, and achievements as well as the financial goals of your telephone fund-raising program and how the money raised will be used.

To get the new callers involved in the learning process and to clear up misconceptions, ask them what they know about the organization and its needs. This sharing of information should last no longer than a half hour. Do not make the mistake of telling new callers too many facts about your organization. They will remember little, if anything, if you do. Callers do not need to know everything about your organization to be top-notch negotiators. Although you need a lot of skill to be an effective fund raiser, you only need a little knowledge. As we said before, once you learn how to negotiate, you can raise funds for any organization.

There is one exception to the rule that you need only a little knowledge and a lot of skill: political telephone fund raising. When you do political telephone fund raising, educating the callers about the issues is nearly as important as teaching them how to negotiate. If the callers are not conversant with the issues, they will not be able to convince the vacillating public to join your side. Your callers must be familiar both with your positions on the issues and those of the opposition. They need to be able to convince potential contributors that your side not only is a good one, but also that it is the better one.

(At the end of training, you will give each caller a fact sheet about your organization. Do not give them this in the morning. If callers receive information in writing, they will not concentrate as hard. You want them to have the information in their heads, not in their hands.)

After you have given the callers some knowledge, it is time to concentrate on developing their negotiating skills. Most callers will have no idea how telephone fund raising really works so have two experienced callers do a role play of a call. One will be the caller and the other will be the potential contributor. The role play enables new callers to grasp the whole before they discuss the parts.

During the role play, the caller should not get off easily. The potential contributor should be recalcitrant enough so that the caller needs to work. But the role play is not a vehicle for super callers to show off. The object is not to scare the new callers away, convinced that they will never become as glib or as resourceful as those who did the role play. The object is to give the new callers an example of a typical call. Make sure that the new callers realize that in a short time they will be just as good as the people who did the role play.

Now, hand out the scripts. Before you discuss the mechanics of the script and its theoretical underpinnings, give your callers about ten minutes to look it over. In addition, have the two experienced callers do a second role play while the new callers follow them using the script. Training is a balance between the theoretical and the practical. It is best to preface the theoretical with the practical: theory only makes sense when put into context.

At this point, you will need to reinstill confidence in your new callers. If you hired correctly, they are ambitious achievers who are accustomed to success. Many now may begin to hesitate, wondering, "Can I do this?" Do not wait for them to ask this question or for uncomprehending looks. Explain that most people begin to have doubts just about then, but emphasize that those doubts will be removed, one by one, as training continues.

After this brief hiatus, it is time to break the script apart, section by section, and analyze each part with the help of the new callers. First, discuss the introduction. This should take no more than a few minutes. Make sure the callers understand that the introduction is standard.

Next, you come to the heart of training, a discussion of the negotiation process. Begin by explaining the importance of starting the negotiation process with a large request: if you do not ask for big pledges, then you will not get them. Starting high also gives the callers a great deal of negotiating room.

The new callers will notice immediately that the script is not as direct during the negotiation process as it is in the introduction. Explain why: because negotiations differ with each call, it is impossible to provide exact wording. All that the script can do with regard to negotiations is provide parameters. Callers will understand this after you discuss the 20 keys to good negotiating, so do this next.

1. Discuss the importance of asking for a specific dollar amount. In other words, discuss why it is that if callers do not ask for a specific dollar amount, they will end up with little or nothing. Also discuss the rule's corrollaries, why callers should never ask potential contributors if they want to pledge, for example. Do not give this rule or its corollaries short shrift. This is *the* most important negotiating key. If callers do not ask for a specific dollar amount, all the other negotiating tactics in the world will mean nothing.

2. Discuss the benefits of using installments—to make large pledges manageable—and how to use them. Discuss the way your particular installment program is structured: what size pledges must be to justify their being paid in installments, when installments will fall due (semiannually, quarterly, monthly), and so on. There must be uniformity in the way callers use installments; for example, one caller cannot offer potential contributors a monthly payment plan for a $100 pledge while another offers them a quarterly payment plan for the same amount. The parameters of the installment option are in the script. Point this out to the callers.

3. Discuss the importance of breaking down a pledge, which is, of course, that it shows potential contributors that you are not asking for the world after all. Next, tell callers how to break down a pledge. Ask them to come up with graphic comparisons of their own; for example, while a dollar a week is less than the price of a Sunday paper, it also is less than the price of a gallon of milk. Show them in the script (in the negotiating chart) where these comparisons are specifically stated. Tell them to feel free to add their own comparisons.

4. Tell the callers that after they use installments and break down the pledge they should restate the specific dollar amount. Although it is important that the caller make the pledge seem manageable to the potential contributor, it is also important that he make very clear the total amount he is asking for.

After you discuss these four rules, have the callers break up into pairs so they can practice what they have just learned, using the script and switching roles so each person has a chance to be the caller. Give them 15 minutes to practice. Ideally, each pair would have a facilitator, someone to coach them while they practice. Of course, this is not possible, but it is possible for you and your two experienced callers (the ones who did so well on the role plays) to circulate around the room giving advice.

It should be clear by now that the two experienced callers are important during training: not only do they help training come alive by doing role plays, but they also help give new callers individual attention. Do not expect them to give up a Saturday or Sunday without compensation. Pay them their regular hourly rate. You should have no trouble attracting callers who will enjoy having the chance to shine and to earn extra money at the same time. Now, back to the rules.

5. Discuss how to control the dialogue. It is important that new callers understand how critical it is to control the conversation at all times. If a caller surrenders control, she never will get a large pledge and, besides, she will waste precious time while the potential contributor rambles on.

Focus in particular on how callers can regain control of the conversation when a potential contributor offers small after they ask big. Explain why they need not accept the small offer. A small offer need not be accepted because it can be inoffensively upgraded using the right negotiating techniques. Role play extensively with this one. It is tough, perhaps the toughest of all negotiating tactics. Have the two experienced callers demonstrate it. Then, have the callers again pair off to practice, while the three of you circulate.

Next, let your callers know that it is all right to interrupt a long-winded caller. Then tell them how to do it.

Finally, discuss why callers must avoid long pauses; that is, so there are no gaps in the conversation that let the potential contributor gain control.

6. Stress how vital it is to assume that everyone can pledge, but do not come straight out and say this. Instead, ask the new callers which groups they think can give and which groups they think cannot give. Your primary interest, of course, is in who they think cannot give. If they are like most new callers, they will tell you that old people probably cannot afford to give. They will tell you to ignore young people, students, and recent graduates as well. If the callers do not come up with these suggestions on their own, guide them by asking questions such as, "Do you think young people can give?" If they are like most new callers, they will tell you that the people who can afford to give are wealthy, middle-aged businessmen.

After you have led them on, it is time to set them straight. Tell them once. Tell them twice. They must assume that everyone can give! Wealthy people become old. Wealth and old age are not mutually exclusive, nor are wealth and youth. There are many young, successful entrepreneurs. There are many young people with inherited wealth, also. Emphasize that there is no surer way to lose money than to assume that someone cannot give.

7. Let the callers know that they should assume that everyone *wants* to give, just as they assume that everyone *can* give. As you know, callers often erroneously assume that unless a potential contributor is enthusiastic, he is uninterested. Make sure that your new callers understand that lack of enthusiasm does not mean lack of interest. The only time to assume that a potential contributor is uninterested is when she says so.

After you are convinced that the new callers understand this, ask them how they would respond to a caller who says, "Listen, I'm just not interested." Guide the discussion to the answer, which is, of course, to provide the potential contributor with information about your organization, stressing the connection between your goals and his self-interest.

Also, stress how important it is that the callers be enthusiastic. Let them know that just as you hope your enthusiasm will carry over to them, their enthusiasm will carry over to the potential contributors. This brings up a critical point: you must maintain your own enthusiasm throughout training. Generating enthusiasm is easy at the start of training. It becomes more difficult as the hours pass. This is why it is important that the new callers participate. When they are talking, you can relax a bit.

8. Discuss the importance of emphasizing mutual self-interest. Begin by asking the new callers why they think people give to worthwhile organizations in general. As usual, guide the conversation toward the logical conclusion. In this case, that logical conclusion is this: people give because it is in their self-interest. Then ask callers why it will be in the best interest of potential contributors to give to your organization in particular. Why will they benefit if you thrive? After the most obvious reasons have come out, encourage the callers to stretch their minds. They should discuss not only why a businessman in the center of town will benefit, but also why a mother of four in the suburbs will benefit, for example. After all, both these people are potential contributors. Let callers know that it is to their advantage to bring up self-interest again and again during a single negotiation. Self-interest is the number one reason why potential contributors give.

9. Explain to the new callers why it is important to make friends

with potential contributors. The reason is obvious. If a potential contributor likes you, he is more likely to help you by pledging. Next, discuss
how to make friends with potential contributors, by inserting their name
now and then into the dialogue, for example.

This is a good opportunity to get the new callers talking. Do not tell
them your ideas until you have heard theirs. Then, reemphasize the
importance of establishing rapport with potential contributors. If some
callers think it is impossible to make friends during a short phone call,
assure them that once they begin to call, this technique, which sounds
difficult, will become second nature.

10. Next, discuss how to assuage irritated potential contributors.
This is another instance when you do not want to blurt out the rule
abruptly. Lead the callers into it by telling them that occasionally a
potential contributor will become irritated by their persistence. Ask
them how they would handle this delicate situation. More specifically,
ask them how they would respond if they were confronted with, "Listen, I understand what you are trying to do, but you are pushing me too
far!" Most new callers will suggest that you apologize profusely. When
you ask them what to do after that, most will tell you that obviously you
should end the call and that someone who is irritated certainly will
never give you money.

Well, the callers are partly right because you need to assuage the
potential contributor before you will get any money from him. But make
it clear to them that after they apologize they must return immediately to
negotiations as usual. Call on your two experienced callers once more to
role play this problem. As the caller becomes more persistent, the potential contributor should become more irritated. Eventually, the potential
contributor should voice his displeasure with the caller's persistence,
giving the caller the opportunity to apologize and return to negotiations.

You have a choice now: either have the callers break up into pairs to
practice this or practice it within the group by asking for volunteers to
role play this tough situation. Only a few confident people will volunteer. All the better. They are the people who will do it best and so will
instill the more reticent new callers with confidence.

11. Discuss the favorable tax consequences that potential contributors will realize from a gift to your organization. Here, the method of
presentation will differ dramatically; you will do almost all the talking.
First, tell the new callers in general terms how potential contributors
benefit from the tax laws. For example, if pledges are tax deductible, tell
them this. (Although most of the new callers will understand the concept of tax-deductibility, some may not, so explain it clearly.) Let the
callers know that they should emphasize the tax consequences of a
pledge, especially at the higher levels of giving. If the training is being

held near the end of the year in October, November, or December, emphasize this even more strongly, because during those months many potential contributors will have seen their accountants and are waiting for your call.

12. Explain how the timing of a gift may be vitally important to your organization. Again, you will do most of the talking. For example, explain that the end of your fiscal year is coming up and your organization needs to know how much money it has to allocate to various programs in the new year. Or, point out that the election is less than a month away and that if your candidate loses, he will not have another chance to run for two more years.

Make sure the new callers realize that stressing timing is not a technique to be used occasionally. Almost every potential contributor needs a push so he will pledge now, not later.

13. Mention that some potential contributors will need reassurance that their money will go for the purpose for which it is given. Show how it is easy to slip this into the conversation with "... and, by the way, your contribution will go directly toward maintaining hiking trails, Mr. Sperry."

At this point, some of the new callers will begin to wonder if they have bitten off more than they can chew. You have told them to emphasize mutual self-interest, to emphasize favorable tax consequences, to emphasize timing, and to emphasize that the pledge will go for the purpose intended. How and when is all this emphasizing possible? Even if your callers do not voice this concern, address it. Ask them to take out their scripts. Show them how much of this information already has been incorporated into the script. Also point out that the script is written to allow callers the freedom to add information as needed and that with time they will be able to weave this information into the script almost by rote. By now, the callers probably are thinking more about their stomachs than their heads, so break for lunch.

What to Do during Lunch

Provide a simple lunch for the new callers. Do not forget the caffeine. You want to make sure they have enough energy for the second half of the day, which will be just as full, if not more so, as the morning. Lunch can give the callers an opportunity to vent their anxiety, but it can only do this if the director is not there. The callers need an opportunity to be completely candid, but you need to insure that they do not panic. Once again, your trusted, experienced callers are the answer. They can assure the worried new callers that with time and practice they will become expert negotiators. They can casually let the new callers know that although telephone fund raising is not easy, it is not as difficult as it may seem at the moment.

Job training, in general, is overwhelming. Training to do telephone fund raising is no exception. Although you do not want to give a watered-down training to make telephone fund raising seem easy, you should not ignore caller anxiety. An hour-long lunch—with the experienced callers there to subtly and casually give encouragement—should lower the anxiety level considerably.

What to Do in the Afternoon

Your revived and reassured callers are ready now to absorb more information. Back to the negotiating rules.

14. Instruct the callers to speak only to the potential contributor herself. Let the callers give you their reasons why this makes good negotiating sense. At the end of the conversation, summarize all their suggestions and add your own, if they missed any.

15. Then discuss how to avoid call backs. New callers assume that when someone asks to be called back he is on the verge of pledging, but needs only a little time to decide how much. You know better. Call backs rarely are profitable.

Take advantage of the callers' renewed energy and begin this discussion by posing a question: "What should you do when confronted with a potential contributor who asks to be called back?" They key is to stress timing vigorously, of course. Earlier you assured the callers that knowing when and where to use tactics like this would become second nature. Now some of them probably will demonstrate that this process already has begun. They accurately will say in answer to your question that the way to avoid call backs is to stress timing. Divide the callers into pairs so they can practice both getting to the potential contributor and avoiding call backs.

16. Discuss credit card pledges in general. Point out that the advantage to the potential contributor is that a credit card pledge allows him to spread out payment of his pledge as he wishes. Point out that the advantage to your organization is that you get the money immediately. Let the callers know that the credit card option is not only a negotiating tool, but also can be used after the pledge is made to insure immediate payment.

17. Now it is time to discuss how callers should deal with dissatis-

fied potential contributors. This will take time, perhaps close to half an hour. Get the callers themselves involved early on by asking them what they would do if a potential contributor raised a complaint about your organization. This should lead to a discussion of the three-step approach that we recommend: recognize the validity of the complaint, explain your position, and then ask for money. Just as we explained to you earlier why each step is important, you must explain the steps and their importance to the new callers. If you are doing political or issue-oriented telephone fund raising, you also will need to discuss how to respond to those who are philosophically opposed to your organization: politely but quickly end the call.

After you discuss how to deal with complaints in general, particularize the discussion. Concentrate on the complaints that the callers are likely to hear. If your program has been going on for a while, you will know what these specific complaints are. If your program is brand-new, concentrate on the generic complaints that every organization has to contend with: "I resent being called at home in the evening," "I don't like to make a commitment over the phone," "I never receive any mail from your organization other than requests for money," and so on. (Do not worry. As soon as your telephone fund-raising program begins to roll, you will quickly discover what the specific complaints are and can tackle them.)

At this point, hand out the Common Problems sheet. You have seen a sample of this before on page 23. Notice that it includes problems that are generic as well as problems that are specific for certain organizations. Go over the Common Problems sheet with the callers. Let them know that it will not provide them with answers to every problem, but it certainly will make handling the common problems easier.

Now it is time to bring out the experienced callers for another role play. This time the potential contributor will be extremely recalcitrant, raising complaint after complaint. The caller will deal with these complaints professionally, relying heavily but not exclusively on the Common Problems sheet. This will show the new callers how easy it is to use the two—the script and the Common Problems sheet—together. Tell the new callers that most potential contributors will not be as recalcitrant, but that you wanted to demonstrate the worst so that normal calls would seem easy.

After the role play, break up the callers into pairs and let them practice dealing with complaints. You and your two helpers will meander around the room, listening and giving advice.

Before moving on to the next rule, warn the new callers not to take complaints personally. They cannot afford tender feelings. An overly sensitive caller is an unproductive caller. In addition, instruct the new callers never to take a nasty remark from a potential contributor personally. In most cases, the remark will be aimed at the organization, not at them. They should respond, therefore, as representatives of the organization, not as individuals.

On the other hand, callers have the right to end the phone call abruptly (not angrily) if a potential contributor becomes highly offensive. If he becomes sexually suggestive or is hot-tempered and begins to rant, the caller should get off the phone, saying in a firm but detached voice, "I am going to end this call." Immediately after saying this, the caller should put down—not slam down—the receiver. Then he should notify the director, who may want to make a short memo about the incident and certainly will want to give the caller comforting support.

Caller abuse almost never happens, but callers should know what to do if it does. Never should callers respond confrontationally. They are paid to negotiate, not to argue.

Arguing with an offensive potential contributor is not good for the program or for the caller. For example, once in a racially tense city, a caller became incensed about what he perceived to be a bigoted remark from a potential contributor. He responded in anger, and the dispute escalated. Ultimately, the caller did hang up, but not until both he, his neighboring caller, and the potential contributor were thoroughly upset. Result: the views of the potential contributor probably did not change one iota, but for the two callers, usually superb negotiators, there was no chance of bonus money that night. Their nerves were jangled and their negotiating skills shot.

18. Ask the callers how they would approach a potential contributor who said that he had other giving priorities. A few probably will suggest that they show the potential contributor why their own organization is better. Praise their spirit, but warn them: callers dare not disparage the competition. Show them how this can backfire. Then tell them what they should do: stress the merits of their own organization. Let them know, as we let you know, that the distinction between tooting your own horn and bad-mouthing the opposition is critical.

19, 20. If your organization has decided to use clubs and/or premiums, discuss them now. Refer the new callers to the negotiating chart in the script which contains all the substantive information they need to know about clubs and/or premiums.

As you will recall, we were hesitant to endorse the use of clubs and premiums broadly. As you will learn, one of the reasons for our hesitation is that callers tend to overemphasize them. It is easier to discuss what the potential contributor will receive than to discuss what he should give. So if you decide to use clubs and/or premiums, make sure your callers realize that they are not the heart of negotiations, simply an added touch. To make this point, ask the callers a rhetorical question such as, "How many of you would give $200 to get an umbrella?"

Now it is time for the new callers to put everything together. Have the two experienced callers do another "packed" role play. This time, as they come up in the role play, explain point by point the negotiating keys that you have just gone over. After the role play, divide the callers into pairs so they can practice. (Of course, each time the new callers form into pairs, they should have different partners, assigned if necessary. This will give them a taste of dealing with all kinds of people, just what they will be required to do on the phone.) Give each caller two sheets of paper, each of which gives a profile of the potential contributor who she is to pretend to be. For example:

> You are a suburbanite who would like to support public broadcasting. Your children grew up on *Sesame Street*. You and your spouse love *Nova* and *Masterpiece Theatre*. But money is tight. You also are annoyed because you did not receive the premium you were promised when you made a contribution last year. As soon as the caller asks you for money, raise your complaint about the premium. If the caller deals with your complaint and is persuasive, pledge $100.

Because each new caller receives two potential contributor profiles, there will be a total of four practice calls per two-person unit. Of course, each profile will raise different problems. This practice will take approximately half an hour.

We have indicated times during training when it is appropriate for the callers to break into pairs to do a role play. You may want to add even more role plays. For example, if the callers seem confused about any of the negotiating tactics, 10 to 15 minutes of role play usually clarifies the point.

Next, briefly discuss deferred due dates. Explain the limited circumstances under which they can be used: when the potential contributor requests the deferral; when the length of the deferral is reasonable; and when the caller obtains the director's permission.

The training is now almost over. Congratulate the callers. Even though you have made it your business to instill confidence in them throughout the workshop, they will welcome still more encouragement.

Next, hand out a one- or two-page synopsis of the most pertinent

Important Facts about the Art Museum

Location:	1014 Westbrook Street Lancole, Wisconsin (Near Exit 7 of Route 13 West)
Budget:	$400,000
Funding sources:	30% comes from the government 25% comes from corporations 10% comes from area businesses 35% comes from the community
Community programs:	Art for tots Adult education classes Free tours of the museum Summer art program for teenagers
Exhibit information:	345-9090
General information:	345-9091
Program information:	345-9098

facts about your organization so that callers will not flounder when asked specific questions. Label each point for quick reference. The fact sheet must be readable. Callers must be able to spot and use the information at a glance, otherwise the fact sheet will be useless during negotiations. Samples are shown on this page and on page 77. One is for an art museum and the other is for a candidate for the school board. Political fund raisers need to know not only about their candidate, but also about the opposition's candidate as well. They need two fact sheets: one giving biographical data about their candidate and the other delineating where the candidates stand on the issues. Give the callers information about current exhibits, current programs, and the like on a separate fact sheet, using colored paper. That way, when these current offerings change, you can simply print up the new information on paper of a different color and exchange the new sheets for the old. The colored paper enables you to tell at a glance whether a caller is using the current fact sheet or an outdated one.

In addition to handing out the fact sheets, hand out a list of the personnel policies. Although the personnel policies are self-explanatory, discuss them anyway. It is important that you make your expectations known in a public way. These policies will be discussed later. Because the personnel policies address potential problems, you must take care not to present them too negatively. If you overemphasize the consequences of unacceptable behavior or of poor performance, the confidence you instilled in callers during training will be undermined. Let the

Important Facts about James Nicklin

Born:	Decatur, Illinois, 1930
Education:	B.A., University of Illinois M.A., University of Chicago
Military service:	Lt., U.S. Army Served in Korean Conflict
Family:	Father of four, all educated in the Decatur public schools. Mrs. Nicklin has been the president of the Decatur Regional High School PTA for the last two years.
Affiliations:	Rotary Club; Veterans of Foreign Wars; Booster Club of Decatur Regional High Schoo; Deacon, Gloria Dei Lutheran Church
Political experience:	Jim has served the Decatur community for the past eight years as a Republican committeeman.

callers know that you have full faith in their ability and that you expect no problems to arise.

At the end of training, the callers will have four handouts: the script, the Common Problems sheet, the fact sheet, and the list of personnel policies. The first three are the only handouts that your callers will need when they telephone. More than this number will be confusing, rather than helpful. Do not make the mistake of inundating the callers with paper.

How Nicklin and Bunnell Compare on the Issues

Issues	James Nicklin	Dorothy Bunnell
Taxes	Opposes any increase in local taxes	Supports proposed increase in local taxes
Library	Opposes expansion. Believes current facilities are adequate	Favors expansion. Expansion will cost $800,000
Closing of the middle school	Favors consolidation of schools to balance city budget	Opposes closing any school
Teachers' salaries	Favors freeze	Supports union demand for 8% increase
Upgrading computer training facilities	Favors	Favors

Close the training with words of encouragement. Let the new callers know that training is ongoing for everyone in the calling coterie. Specifically, let them know that they will receive plenty of help and that you do not expect perfection at the beginning. Add that you have a good feeling about their group and are sure they are winners, every one.

During training, there was no discussion of paperwork because callers would never remember it. As you will learn, an assistant will help you supervise the session. He will meet with callers before their first calling session to explain the paperwork and to give them one final pep talk.

There was also no discussion of the negotiating taboos which were covered on pages 28 through 29. Most callers would not think of these questionable tactics on their own. Mentioning them may plant ideas in their heads. This is one case where it is better to handle the problem when and if it occurs rather than to try to prevent it. By trying to prevent it, you may actually encourage it.

Finally, there was no discussion of the offensive mannerisms (using profanity, for example), which were covered on pages 29 through 30. As with the negotiating taboos, take care of these when and if the need arises.

Truncated Training

As you will recall, we explained that extremely short one-shot deals as well as political campaigns close to election day probably will have to do without an all-day training. Instead, they will have to give truncated trainings. The best time to give a truncated training is immediately before the callers' first calling session.

As you now know, training is an intricate blend of presentation, demonstration, discussion, and practice. If training is shortened to two hours, for example, you will not be able to have such a healthy and productive mix of learning techniques. You can do without demonstration, discussion, and practice, if you must. You cannot do without presentation, obviously. Callers must be taught how to negotiate.

After spending no more than ten minutes telling them the bare facts about your organization and why it needs money, hand out the scripts. Let the callers read them. Then, plunge into a discussion of the negotiating rules. You will not have time to ask questions or to involve the callers in dialogue. You simply will have to tell them the basic negotiating rules, disregarding many of the subtleties.

Because you will be spending no more than ten minutes telling new callers the facts about your organization, you probably will need to prepare a fact sheet presenting in written form the same information that you would present orally in a full-length training. This will be especially necessary during political telephone fund raising, when callers need facts about the opposition as well as facts about the organization for which they are calling. Keep this information well-organized and readable or it will be ignored.

Even with only a truncated training, your callers will do better than you ever dreamed. We have shown you how to train a coterie of perfect callers. Of course, the more perfect the calling coterie, the more productive the program. But even if your callers fall somewhat short of perfection, they still will be able to negotiate handsome pledges.

Monitoring Callers

Training is only the first step in developing a coterie of excellent callers. Telephone fund raising requires extensive on-the-job training. You will need to work with your callers continually.

By looking at the callers' totals each evening, you will get a good idea of who is doing well and who is not, but you will not know why. The best way to help your callers improve is to listen to their calls so you can diagnose their weaknesses and make appropriate recommendations. Everything that follows in this section applies to volunteer and paid callers without distinction.

Mechanics

You will need a monitoring system—a device that allows you to listen to calls while they are in progress. A traditional Call Director with as many buttons as there are phones in the calling room is a sensible choice. You can rent one from the phone company. To monitor calls without being detected, simply unscrew the part of the handset that you talk into. That way, when you see a caller's line light up on the Call Director, you can listen in unobtrusively.

There are two alternatives to using a monitoring device. One alternative is to ask the caller what happened during a given call. Most callers cannot report accurately what happened. Even the most honest callers see their calls quite differently from the way they actually occur. The other alternative is to have a supervisor walk around the calling room and listen to the calls. The problem with this approach is that the supervisor can get only half the picture, and, as we just mentioned, you cannot count on your callers to provide the other half. Neither alternative is satisfactory. You need to hear both sides of the conversation to know what really is going on.

Privacy

Being monitored is unsettling, even for the most experienced callers. Callers often tend to see monitoring as an invasion of their privacy. But attitudes toward privacy are based on expectations, so set these expectations in training and in your personnel policies. Let the callers know that you will monitor their calls periodically. Emphasize how this will help them. Let them know that by working with them to remove negotiating weaknesses, you increase the likelihood that they will be able to earn more. If you explain the purpose of monitoring to the callers at the outset, you will have few problems. If you view the procedure as helpful, so will they.

Make monitoring easier by keeping track of where callers sit. Draw a simple map of the calling room, indicating the phone number at each seat. Run off copies, then fill in the callers' names at each session. By the way, date and save these maps just in case a dispute arises about unauthorized use of the phones.

Who Should Be Monitored

Everyone should be monitored: new callers, experienced callers, bad callers, and good callers. While you should monitor all callers, the way in which you approach them about this and the frequency with which you monitor them will depend on their status.

New callers should be monitored their first night on the job and if not then, no later than the second night. Bad habits solidify quickly.

Let your callers know that at the beginning you will monitor them as often as possible. New callers usually appreciate this. They want their job. You will help them keep it.

As soon as you have an idea what a new caller's strengths and weaknesses are, call him into your office. Sometimes this will occur after listening to only one call. Other times you will need to listen to a series of calls before you can make an assessment.

When you have the caller in your office for the first time, reiterate the purpose of the monitoring process: to help, not to hinder. Go over the call(s) in detail. Make sure that the caller knows which call(s) you are discussing with him. It is as important to tell him what he did right as it is to tell him what he did wrong. When discussing specific negotiating weaknesses, be direct. Tell the caller exactly what he did wrong and how he can improve. For example:

Your discussion of the installment option at the $200 level was unclear. You asked the potential contributor for $50 quarterly. Now, I know what you meant. You know what you meant. But I don't think the potential contributor knew what you meant. What you should have said was, "How about a pledge of $200, which you can pay in four quarterly installments of $50?"

or

You did a beautiful job of weaving the installment option throughout the call. You also used the background information perfectly. I think you convinced the potential contributor that we are at least as worthy as the other organizations that he is supporting. Next call, however, try to remember to break down the pledge for the potential contributor, as well. Let him know, for example, that a pledge of $50 is less than $1 a week.

In addition to going over negotiating strategies with the caller, point out his mannerisms. For example, interjections of "you know" or "okay?" are not acceptable when used habitually.

At this point, it should be clear that because you will be going over the calls in great detail, you will need to take notes. The best way to do this is discussed later in the chapter. If a caller asks to see your notes, share them with him readily. It is always wise to treat the callers with respect, to be open and frank with them.

After discussing the strengths and weaknesses of the call(s), conclude your conversation with words of encouragement. Reiterate the positive points. Let the caller know you are confident that he can overcome the weaknesses. Remind him to come to you if he needs help, adding that of course you will continue to monitor him so you can gauge his progress.

No matter how well you screen applicants, sometimes you will hire the wrong person. Every once in a while, you will listen to a new caller who performs as if he never attended training. Let this caller go immediately. Fair callers can become good callers, but poor callers can become no more than mediocre. You do not have time to cultivate mediocre callers. It is better to spend time turning fair callers into good callers and good callers into excellent callers. When you come across this situation, tell the caller exactly how you feel. Let him know that telephone fund raising is not for everyone, and that while you are sure he has many strengths, telephone fund raising obviously is not one of them. Then dismiss him. A caller who is let go after his first evening of calling should not be completely surprised. Your personnel policies should expressly state that you reserve the right to let any caller go after the first session, and you should mention this at the training.

Do not remonitor a new caller immediately. That would imply a lack of confidence. Give the new caller a day or two to try to implement the negotiating suggestions that you made. Then remonitor him.

When you call him into your office a second time, refresh his memory about the strengths and weaknesses of his previous calls. Let him know which strengths still apply. (Quite possibly, they all do.) Let him know whether he has corrected his weaknesses. Where improvement has been made, extend your pleasure. Where improvement is still needed, make directive suggestions. Also discuss any additional weaknesses you have discovered.

If the caller made no progress after your first meeting, let him go. Your loss is not only the money you pay an unproductive caller as salary, but also the money that the caller fails to raise. Therefore, let the caller go even if he is a volunteer.

After the second meeting, it is time to hand out praise to those who show promise. This is when the callers need it most. They have been calling just long enough to discover that negotiating takes all the moxie they can muster.

Even when your callers are no longer new, they still need to be monitored, but the focus and frequency of the monitoring will differ. The purpose of monitoring experienced callers is not to teach but to refine. They all can improve: good callers can become excellent; excellent callers, superlative. Experienced callers will be monitored less frequently then are new callers, naturally.

Experienced callers usually are less receptive to monitoring than are new callers. They tend to view it as interference. Although you explained the monitoring process in training, your words may have faded from their minds. That is why you need to approach experienced callers as follows.

Invite the caller into your office. Let her know how pleased you are with her progress. Also, let her know you believe that she has yet to reach her full potential. Stress that the better she does, the more money she will earn and that you would like to help her by listening to a few of her calls.

Why do you tell the caller in advance that you plan to listen to her calls? It is a courtesy. It demonstrates your respect for her. It lets her know that you trust her and that you are simply trying to help her.

You will need to prioritize which experienced callers to monitor. The following groups should receive preference:

First, relatively new callers should still receive priority. The more experience a caller has, the less monitoring he will need. Conversely, the less experience a caller has, the more monitoring he will need.

Second, slumping callers should receive some priority. One or two unproductive nights does not constitute a slump. Four or five probably does. If a caller is slumping, begin by telling him you believe that he is an able telephone fund raiser, but add that you realize he is in a slump. Let him know you plan to listen to a few of his calls to figure out what is going wrong. Callers may be in a slump because of personal problems or problems with their other job. Slumping callers frequently are frustrated and on-edge. Be sensitive to this when you approach them.

Third, if you suspect that a caller is dishonest, monitor her immediately, no matter what her level of experience. Do not give advance warning. If she is doing something dishonest—falsifying pledges, for example—she certainly will not do it if she knows you are listening in. If you discover that your suspicions were correct, let her go at once. Dishonesty is contagious; nip it in the bud.

Of course, top-notch callers have a low priority for monitoring. Nonetheless, monitor them occasionally just to make sure they are doing as well as they possibly can. Be prepared for a few prima donnas. A highly competitive caller once complained bitterly about being monitoried, insisting that he was being monitored so that the director could discover what his techniques were and share them with less productive callers. Clearly written personnel policies come to the rescue. He had known all along that every caller—new and old—is monitored periodically.

To make the monitoring process more concrete, we have included a sample phone call and an evaluation of that call. As you read the dialogue, take notes on the caller's strengths and weaknesses then compare your evaluation with ours.

CALLER: Hello, this is Mark DiFelice calling from Alpha Beta Gamma for Dan Gorman.

POTENTIAL CONTRIBUTOR: Hello, this is Dan. What can I do for you?

CALLER: I'd like to speak with you for a few moments about Alpha Beta Gamma.

POTENTIAL CONTRIBUTOR: I'm very familiar with ABΓ. I've been an active member ever since I moved to the Bay Area.

CALLER: I'm glad to hear that, Dan. Then you probably know that we're trying to raise $50,000 to renovate the old Horton Hotel as a shelter and clinic for the homeless.

POTENTIAL CONTRIBUTOR: Listen, let me save you some time. I'd love to help. But I just took on a big mortgage. My own home is the only home I can worry about, at least for a while. But, because I want to support the fraternity in this, I'll give you $50.

CALLER: Thank you very much for your offer of $50! But this year we need a little more. How about giving us that pledge four times a year for a total of $200. That would make you a member of the ABΓ Council.

Caller Evaluation

Caller: *MARK DIFELICE*

Date: *NOVEMBER 10, 1986*

Monitor: *GIGI BARRETT*

- good recovery after potential contributor interrupted
- correctly tried to upgrade $50 offer to $200
- failed to stress peer involvement or timing
- didnt break pledge down
- installment option unclear at $200 level
- no validation

POTENTIAL CONTRIBUTOR: If I could, I would. But if $50 isn't enough, take nothing.

CALLER: I'm sorry. I didn't mean to suggest that $50 wasn't enough. All we need right now is $50. Could you give us $50 now and then again in six months?

POTENTIAL CONTRIBUTOR: I won't commit six months in advance. $50—take it or leave it.

CALLER: We'll take it. Thanks so much.

POTENTIAL CONTRIBUTOR: Will you send me a form, or do you have an address where I should send my check?

CALLER: We will send you a pledge confirmation tomorrow. Enclosed will be a postage-paid return envelope. Thank you again.

Things to heed about the evaluation sheet: (1) strengths as well as weaknesses were noted; (2) the points were listed in the only logical way—chronologically; (3) just enough information was listed to remind the director of the points she wants to discuss with the caller; and (4) the evaluation sheet itself is very simple. Do not bother developing a complex monitoring sheet. Taking simple notes, like those illustrated, works best.

File your evaluation sheets. They document performance. Therefore, they provide the information you will need to decide who to let go and to whom to give raises.

If a caller performs very poorly and you think you may have to let her go, take a few minutes after the call to note her weaknesses in greater detail. Then confer with the caller and discuss these weaknesses thoroughly. After the conference, ask her to sign the evaluation sheet. These steps will insure that the caller understands why she was let go, if it comes to that. They also will insure that you have documentation of her understanding.

Supervising Callers

Although monitoring is the most important part of supervision, other things must be done as well if the calling session is to run smoothly. The list is extensive. No director can adequately perform all these tasks alone. Therefore, every director, unless he has only a handful of callers, will need supervisory help during the calling session.

Note that although the supervisory role will be divided between the director and the assistant, this section uses the word "supervisor" as if the tasks were performed by one person.

Motivating the Callers before the Session

One important function of the supervisor is to energize the callers, who may have hurried in after an exhausting day at work or school. There are a number of good ways to motivate the callers at the beginning of the session before calling actually begins.

1. Give the callers a five- to ten-minute pep talk before they begin to call, telling them how well they are doing compared with last month, talking to them about specific negotiating techniques if they seem to have forgotten them, explaining an urgent need of the organization, and so on. These pep talks are fun for the supervisor. It is pleasant to have a captive audience. Despite this, only give them when the callers need them. It may mean giving them every day. It may mean giving them once a week.

2. Discuss negotiating techniques and common problems, involving the entire group in the discussion. Unlike the pep talk, here the supervisor plays the role of facilitator rather than orator. He initiates a vigorous discussion by asking questions such as (1) Who do you consider the toughest potential contributors? Why? How do you deal with them? (2) What negotiating technique is most difficult for you? How do you overcome that difficulty?

At these discussions, callers may express concerns that they do not feel comfortable voicing elsewhere, such as anxiety about completing their paper work or annoyance with being monitored. Do not allow the discussion to become a free-for-all, however. The conversation must be guided and should last no longer than 15 to 20 minutes.

Sometimes, it is just as productive to invite four to six people— mixing experienced and inexperienced callers—to meet with the supervisor for a similar discussion during the calling session. Some callers may feel more at ease in a small group.

3. Ask two superior callers to stage a role play of the script for the other callers. Let them practice for a few minutes first, of course. Have one be the caller and the other a recalcitrant potential contributor. After they are through, encourage the other callers to dissect the dialogue. Certainly you will want to do this every time there is a change in the script. Do it more often if it invigorates the callers.

Use all of the above at one time or another. If callers come to work expecting just another pep talk from the director going over familiar techniques, exhorting them to do better and better, a talk during which they can let their minds wander, time is wasted. Even five unproductive minutes multiplied by 20 callers adds up to a long time lost. Keep chang-

ing the method of motivation, therefore, and involve the callers themselves as much as possible.

Inspiring the Callers during the Session

Not only is it important for the supervisor to motivate people before
the session, but it also is important that he keep them motivated during
the session. There are a number of good ways to do this.

1. The supervisor should post high totals as the night rolls along.
As you will learn, the calling room should have at least two chalk
boards. As you also will learn, individual totals as well as large pledges
are important to the callers because they determine who gets bonus
money. Because he continually moves around the room checking the
callers' totals, the supervisor knows who is doing well. Forty-five minutes into the session, he knows, for example, that Lila already has
pledges amounting to $250, that Mike is not far behind with $225, and
that Joe is in the running with $175. The supervisor posts these callers'
names and the dollar amounts on the board. Of course, the names and
amounts change often during the night, and the names of those in
fourth, fifth, and even sixth place will probably be posted as well, especially if the tallies are close. When the supervisor notices a new caller
or someone who usually is not among the winners surging upward, he
will expand the list to include that name. Recognition is important, too,
whether or not it is accompanied by bonus money.
2. The supervisor also should post sizeable pledges, especially if
they come at the start of the evening. If a caller gets off to a fast start, let
everyone know it. For example, the supervisor can write on the chalk-
board, "Craig already has two $50 pledges!" Also announce the pledge
rate and the average pledge, if they are impressive. Let the callers know,
for example, that one out of every three families in Boulder is pledging
and is giving an average of $60.
3. It is perfectly okay to announce aloud the names and totals of
those in the lead, in addition to posting them, especially toward the end
of the session as it becomes more and more of a contest. Calling is hard
work and often tedious. The entire endeavor becomes more interesting
if the supervisor makes the most out of the rivalry for bonus money.

Saving the Session from Disaster

As will be discussed later in this section, the supervisor periodically
gauges the session's productivity. If he discovers that the callers are

having a poor night, there are a number of session-saving measures he can take immediately.

1. The supervisor can stop the calling temporarily to let the callers know that things are not going well: for example, that only $500 has been raised and that usually by then at least twice that much has been raised. This is a good time for the supervisor to get feedback from the callers. What is happening? Together, the group might be able to solve the common problem plaguing nearly every one of them: lack of positive response from potential contributors. Even if no solution is found, a break will help the session start afresh with invigorated callers. Keep this break down to ten minutes or less. Time is precious.
2. In place of stopping the session, which is a drastic measure to use rarely, the supervisor can award impromptu, one-time bonuses announcing, for example, "$2 for each of the next three pledges over $150!"
3. Generally, when things are slow, very slow, both the director and the supervisor should be in the calling room energizing the callers. This is the one time when monitoring takes second place.

Preparing Supplementary Materials

If the supervisor discovers that callers are collectively having difficulty with a particular aspect of negotiations, then, in addition to discussing the problem with the group before calling begins and emphasizing it in subsequent trainings, he should prepare a handout addressing the problem. The following will give you an idea what these sample handouts should be like.

PROBLEM AND SOLUTION 1

Problem

You are discussing a $300 gift with the potental contributor. Naturally, you have told her that this would be tax-deductible, that she could charge this to her credit card, and that this pledge works out to be less than $6 a week. You are about to offer the potential contributor the option of paying the pledge in installments when she says: "Well, I'll give you $50 like I did last year." What do you do now?

Solution

1. Thank the potential contributor for her offer of continued support.

2. Explain why we need an extraspecial commitment this year: our goal is to double the number of volumes in the library.

3. Then ask for more money. Use installments to bridge the gap between your request and her offer.

Illustration

Thank you so much, Mrs. McIntyre, for your offer of $50 and for your continued support. It's just that this year we need a little more. As you may know, our goal is to double the number of volumes in our library by next Christmas. That's why I hope you can give us $50 now and then again three more times throughout the year. Three months would separate each payment. That will make a total pledge of $200. And this pledge is actually less than $4 a week, less than the cost of one movie ticket. Think of it, Mrs. McIntyre, for less than the cost of one movie ticket a week, we offer you and your family a treasure of good literature. And, of course, this contribution would be tax-deductible. How does that sound, Mrs. McIntyre?"

PROBLEM AND SOLUTION 2

Problem

Just as you introduce yourself to the potential contributor, he says, "Are you calling about money? Well, I can't give!" What do you do now?

Solution

As tempting as it is to hang up, don't do it. Despite the potential contributor's opening remarks, you still might be able to get him to pledge. Do the following:

1. Briefly—keep it to a few words—tell him the purpose of your call: to garner support for the library.

2. Tell him how he benefits from our program.

3. Ask him for money.

Illustration

"As a matter of fact, I am calling about money. You know, Mr. Wilheim, without public support, there would be no local library. I'm sure it's important to you, as it is to your neighbors, that you and your children have a well-stocked library nearby. That's why we hope you will support us this year with a pledge of $200, which is actually less than $4 a week. . . ."

The handout, in conjunction with discussion of the problem before the group, should take care of it for all current callers. Because it will be emphasized in subsequent training, it should not be a problem with new callers. However, if the problem resurfaces, a supplementary training may be necessary.

Holding Supplementary Trainings

Upon occasion, the supervisor may need to give a short supplementary training taking between a half hour to an hour. He should give a supplementary training, however, only if what he has to say cannot be covered in a few minutes at the beginning of the session or in a handout. Ideally, the supplementary training will take place before the calling session. It will be cheaper in the long run to pay the callers to come in early then to have a befuddled calling coterie. But if the callers cannot come in early, the supervisor has no choice but to take time off from the calling session itself.

Give a short supplementary training, for example, if callers are having one or two common negotiating problems. Callers may be unable to deal with potential contributors who have complaints about your organization, for instance. Focus on the problem by role playing and brainstorming with the callers. You will be surprised how insightful callers can be when inspired this way. Not only will they leave the retraining confident of their ability to deal with the problem, but they also will have the good feeling that they are part of a team, someone who both sustains and is sustained by the others.

Likewise, give a short supplementary training if there is a major change in your program. Let's say, for example, that your program decides to begin using premiums. You suddenly will have a coterie of novice callers on your hands, novices in the sense that they are totally unskilled in the use of premiums. The callers all will need to know how to weave them into negotiations skillfully. The best way to start is by explaining how the new policy will help them bring in more money. They will listen carefully if they know how personal an interest they have in this. Next, explain the advantages and pitfalls of using premiums. Have the callers break up into twos, so they can role play. Practice and practice, switching partners often. The supervisor will walk around the room picking up weaknesses and giving counseling. Conclude the supplementary training with a question and answer time.

Overseeing the Session

The following are the tasks of the supervisor in his role as overseer:

1. He takes the roll, marking down both absence and lateness.
2. He schedules callers for their next week's work. New callers should start off by calling two nights a week, no more, no less, until they demonstrate that they have a good grasp of the necessary negotiating skills. Some will do this right away and can quickly move up to calling three nights a week. Generally, by calling two nights a week, callers will develop good negotiating skills. By calling two or three nights a week, they will maintain those skills. But, if they call four nights a week, those skills may actually decline as callers become more and more burnt out.
3. He fills out a map of the calling room so the person doing the monitoring can keep track of which phone each caller is using.
4. He distributes potential contributor records to the callers. A potential contributor record is an information sheet giving all the relevant data about the potential contributor. (Details about the potential contributor record are discussed later.) His optimistic comments on the merits of these records as he distributes them ("There's big money in this bunch from Society Hill!" or "These look like good ones. Most of them are from the Main Line!") will warm the callers' hearts. They will respond enthusiastically if they feel that special care was taken to give them winners.
5. He keeps the calling room functioning in a disciplined way. For example, callers will not bring in enough money if they do not complete enough calls. Merely having a supervisor around increases the likelihood that the callers will talk to the potential contributors instead of to one another.

If the supervisor notices that the number of contacts completed each night is falling among a group of callers who always sit together, it may be necessary for him to break up the group. But, as a general rule, callers should be allowed to select their own seats. Most callers do not abuse the privilege of being able to chat with their neighbors between calls. As a matter of fact, most chatter will be work related.

6. He keeps an eye open—discreetly—for sneaky tactics (callers leafing through their stack of potential contributor records, calling only those which look most promising, and then asking for more records, claiming to have called them all, for example).

On the other hand, the supervisor must take great pains to distribute the records equitably. The callers have money at stake. They will be on the alert for favoritism and may erupt if they think it is occurring.

7. He makes sure that ambitious callers do not enter the paper room (where potential contributor records are stored) to help themselves to the most promising ones.

8. He also makes sure that callers do not hoard potential contributor records. Hoarding occurs if a caller notices the name of a generous contributor on one of her potential contributor records, but she cannot contact him that night; so she puts his record away so that she herself can call him later. No one should remove a record from circulation unless instructed to do so. Hoarding could tie up the best potential contributor records indefinitely.

9. Several times during the session, he adds up the total amount of money that has been raised to make sure that the session is progressing as expected. He may check the amount of the average pledge and the pledge rate, in addition. (These terms are discussed later.) When the session is going well, keeping track of and announcing these statistics will energize the callers and make a successful night even better. When the session is going slowly, it is useful for the supervisor to know just how slowly, so he can take swift and appropriate remedial action.

10. He checks periodically on those doing pledge collection to make sure they are working diligently, especially if they are in an out-of-the-way corner or in another room. As you will learn shortly, pledge collection is an integral part of the telephone fund-raising program.

11. He patiently explains the paperwork to new callers before their initial calling session. He shows them how to fill out the potential contributor records and how to keep track of their efforts on the nightly totals sheet, for example. He also makes sure that callers who are not new complete their paper work as well. The supervisor should remind these callers—repeatedly if necessary—that one of their responsibilities is to complete the paperwork. If callers do not complete their paperwork conscientiously in the evening, the clerical staff will not be able to do its work efficiently during the day.

12. He approves deferred due dates sparingly in accordance with the guidelines given on pages 33 through 34. He makes a notation on the potential contributor record indicating his approval.

13. He is flexible enough to adapt his style to the callers' needs: with unruly callers, he is stern; with lazy callers, he is upbeat and energizing; with new callers, he is encouraging. In general, he maintains a calm but assertive presence in the calling room.

Coaching the Callers

While monitoring the callers is the best way to assess their ability, this does not mean that just hearing one side of a conversation is completely without value. At times, a supervisor will overhear the caller's side of a conversation and from that alone will be able to counsel him. If, for example, the supervisor hears the caller ask a potential contributor, "What would you like to give?," he should coach the caller immediately after the call. He should do the same if, for example, he hears the caller presenting the installment option unclearly.

Confirming Pledges

Whenever a caller gets a big pledge, $150, for example, the supervisor will follow it up with a thank-you call. He should do this right after the caller hangs up, so he will be sure to catch the potential contributor at home.

What does this accomplish? First, it makes the contributor feel good about his pledge: a person of stature has taken the time to call. (For this reason, the supervisor should use his title when he calls.)

Second, it makes the contributor realize that the commitment was a firm one. He confirmed it verbally with two people: a caller and the supervisor.

The thank-you call can serve one further purpose. If you are uncertain about the validity of any commitment—large or small—call up and confirm. If the pledge is not valid, you will know this right away and will not waste time and money following it up.

The thank-you call should sound something like this: "Hello, this is (name), (title), from (organization). I couldn't resist calling to thank you personally for your generous support. It is a pleasure to run across people like you who appreciate what we are doing and stand behind us so firmly. Also, I want you to know that we will make every effort to insure that every penny of your contribution goes directly to (mention a facet of your program that you are sure the potential contributor approves of; for example, a public broadcasting station might say "goes directly to programming").

Choosing a Supervisor

The requirements for supervisor are these:

1. He should be able to perform all the supervisory tasks, including monitoring. Therefore, he must be someone who has demonstrated his ability as a caller.
2. He should have an agreeable personality that does not get on the callers' nerves. This is essential, because he needs to be ubiquitous yet inconspicuous.

3. He should be trustworthy. The callers must trust him; otherwise, they might look on him as a management spy plunked down in their midst. The director also must trust him; otherwise, she will not be able to rely on him. For example, he must be able to pass on information about individual callers, putting aside conflicting loyalties. Remember, the supervisor probably will be someone who, until recently, was a caller himself.
4. He should be flexible, so that the director has some leeway as to what roles he would like him to perform on a given evening.
5. He should have a good working relationship with the director. Managing telephone fund raisers is not easy. Working as a team, the director and the supervisor can accomplish miracles that neither could achieve separately.

There is no magic formula for dividing duties between the director and his assistant. Chances are every organization will do it differently. Since the supervisor is a flexible person capable of performing all the supervisory tasks well, the director can assign them to him as necessary. For example, if the director wants to spend an evening in the calling room, the supervisor will monitor. Or, if the director wants to monitor nonstop one evening, the supervisor will take care of everything else.

Paying Your Callers and Supervisors

How to Pay Your Callers

Pay your callers a moderate rate with the chance to earn bonus money. The base pay should be above minimum wage to attract ambitious, energetic people. A good starting point is 75¢ above the minimum wage.

There must be salary mobility. Award raises at a steady pace to callers who bring in money. Caller rankings are discussed later. They, as well as the caller evaluations, will help you decide to whom to give a raise.

Do not put a ceiling on salaries. Recruiting and training are costly. Do not adopt the attitude that callers are easily replaceable. It is cheaper to keep good callers than to find new ones.

In addition to their hourly wage, callers will be eligible for bonus money. Design an incentive system that will encourage them to raise as much money as possible. In other words, reward those who raise the most money each evening. Reward approximately 20% of the calling pool. For example, if you have 18 callers on Monday, reward the top four. If you have 14 on Tuesday, reward only the top three. Give $6 to the best caller, $5 to the second best, and so on.

Do not award nightly bonuses for the total amount of dollars raised to substantially *more than 20%* of your callers. If you do, the bonuses no longer will reward excellence. Do not award nightly bonuses for the total amount of dollars raised to substantially *less than 20%* of your callers. If you do, you run the risk of rewarding the same top callers each evening. The 20% rule accommodates your competing needs to encourage excellence and to insure that a substantial percentage of the calling coterie competes actively for bonus money.

As an alternative, try the following bonus. Determine the dollars raised per session per caller. (You will learn how to make this calculation in Chapter 4 in the section on record keeping.) Multiply that by 1.5. Now you have the bonus threshold. All callers who pass this threshold will receive a bonus of one dollar for each $100 that they raise. For example, if the dollars raised per session per caller is $300, the threshold would be $450. If a caller raises $600, she will receive $6. If she raises $750, she will receive $7. Note that there is no upper limit to this bonus. If a caller raises $1700, for example, she will receive $17. (If she raises only $400, however, she will receive no bonus, even if she is the top caller for the session.)

The advantage of this bonus is that everyone can qualify for it: it provides a broader incentive. The disadvantage is that it reduces competition, which in itself is an incentive.

In addition to rewarding nightly totals, reward large pledges. The parts are as important as the whole; you want to encourage not only high totals but large pledges as well. So, if the average pledge in your program is $50, give the callers 1% of each pledge of $200 or over. For example, a caller would earn a $3 bonus for a $300 pledge.

Introduce additional bonuses to solve immediate problems.

1. If the calling session is off to a slow start, award a bonus to whoever gets the first large pledge—$150 or over, for example. Of course, announce the winner with a flourish.
2. If the evening still seems sluggish, award a bonus to whoever gets the next large pledge—$200 or over, for example. Announce this with a flourish, also.
3. If the callers are not pursuing the credit card option vigorously, award a bonus to the caller who gets the most credit card pledges for the session.
4. If a few talented callers make off with the bonus money night after night despite your attempts to include as many people as possible, bonuses will mean little to most of the callers. To get

everyone involved, have each caller put his name on a slip of paper every time he gets a pledge of $50 or more. A low threshold of $50 makes it easy for mediocre callers to compete. Do not make it difficult to qualify for this bonus; otherwise, only your top callers will enjoy this bonus as well. At the end of the evening, put the slips of paper into a box. Hold a drawing. Award the winner an hour's wage.

As you can see, the callers will have many incentives to negotiate well going on simultaneously. Each bonus need not be large for assertive callers to see the difference in their paychecks. Those little bonuses add up. Of course, discontinue old bonuses that no longer serve their purpose.

In general, bonuses for individual pledges should be paid when the pledge is paid. Do not pay this money when the pledge is made, for this would provide the callers with an incentive to falsify pledges to earn bonus money. But, if the potential contributor has chosen to pay her pledge in installments, pay the caller his bonus after the first installment is received. Do not make your callers wait until each installment is collected. Payment of the first installment is a good signal that the pledge is valid; otherwise, the potential contributor would not have paid it. Moreover, making the callers wait until each installment is collected would discourage them from using the installment option as a negotiating device because it would not work to their immediate financial benefit.

Pay the nightly bonuses immediately. Do not wait until each pledge from a given evening is collected. If you insisted that the callers wait to receive the bonus, this would remove much of the incentive that the bonus system is designed to provide. Equally important, it would make the bonus sytem too complicated to administer. Because this bonus is paid before the money actually comes in, you need to counteract any tendency a caller might have to falsify pledges to gain bonus money. Let your callers know in your personnel policies and during training that if you discover that a caller is falsifying pledges, she will be let go. Also let your callers know that if they falsify pledges, you will eventually learn about it. You will receive complaints from potential contributors who were the victims of their abuse, and you also will discover falsified pledges during pledge collection, which is discussed later.

How to Reward Your Volunteers

Just because you are not paying your volunteers with money, that does not mean they are receiving nothing for their efforts. There are ways to reward people other than by paying them. The following is an illustrative list of ways to pay your volunteers without giving them a check:

1. Your gratitude is one reward. Many people volunteer because they want a sense of belonging. They like being part of a group. Your approval is important to them. Accordingly, take time to coddle them. Give them as much praise and feedback as you possibly can. Pay them the courtesy of acquainting them with units of your organization other than the telephone fund-raising program. Give them a special tour of the building, for example, treating them like the extraordinary people they are.

2. Throw a party at the end of your program or at any monumental point—when you collect your first $100,000, for example. Try to have the food, spirits, and whatever else is needed donated. A good bash builds morale. Your callers will appreciate your going out of the way to insure that they have a good time. In return, they will continue to go out of their way for you in their fund-raising efforts.

3. Grant them privileges, wherever possible. For example, a university might grant them access to its athletic facilities. A political organization might try to provide them with opportunities to meet and talk with the candidate. A theater might sell them tickets at a discount.

4. Recognize their efforts publicly in press releases, newsletters, and the like.

5. Occasionally present them with something to show off similar to the premiums that contributors sometimes receive. For example, a national organization with thousands of volunteers gives its male volunteers a tie after 1000 hours of work and a brandy snifter after 2000 hours. Both the tie and the snifter carry the organization's name, of course.

6. Check the federal and state tax rules. Volunteers can sometimes take sizeable deductions for mileage.

7. A volunteer gains something just by virtue of her involvement: she gains experience. In many cases, volunteers view their efforts, rightfully so, as an investment in their own futures. When you try to recruit volunteers, stress the practical value of the experience. Let them know that you believe the experience is excellent resume material and that you will write recommendations for those volunteers who excel.

8. Volunteers chose your organization out of all the others compet-

ing for their time and skills because your cause is close to their hearts. The satisfaction one gets from working productively for a cause one believes in is a reward that cannot be measured.

How to Pay the Supervisor

The supervisor should be paid twice the hourly rate of new callers. If new callers start at $4 an hour, the supervisor should start at $8 an hour. Most supervisors were once productive callers making a good hourly wage plus bonuses. Good people need a financial incentive to switch from calling to the tougher task of supervising. To make the job even more alluring, present it as a beginning-level management position, one that will be valuable experience for someone who wants to learn how telephone fund raising functions.

Letting Go Unsatisfactory Callers

Along with hiring goes firing, of course. Yes, you will be hiring a good many talented people. You also will be hiring some who do not measure up.

Your first commitment must be to the program and not to any individual caller. If you keep a caller because you have a soft spot for him, in addition to running the risk of being seen as partial (and possibly discriminatory when you let someone else go), you prevent your program from reaching its full potential. Mediocre callers use up good potential contributors, potential contributors who, with the right sort of direction, would give you handsome sums. Accordingly, you owe it to yourself and to the program to fire those callers who are not an asset. If you find firing as distasteful as most do, that is all the more incentive to perform your job of screening thoroughly and to train and coach well.

This section provides you with guidance about how and when to let callers go. Particular emphasis is on legal considerations.

Impermissible Reasons to Fire

Generally, it is illegal, as well as immoral, to fire someone because of race, religion, gender, national origin, age, sexual preference, or handicapped status. In other words, it is illegal to fire someone because of a personal quality that does not relate to her work performance.

For the remainder of this section, we assume, as we must, that you would never let someone go for an impermissible reason, that you would only let someone go because of what they do or do not do at work, not because of who they are.

Document Poor Performance

Sometimes an employee who has been fired will believe that your motivation was improper, however, even though it was not. If you are hiring and firing a great many callers, this is a real but conquerable problem. The employee may threaten to sue or may actually sue. If the employee sues, or if you believe the threat is real, consult an attorney. The following discussion should not be construed as legal advice or opinions concerning specific factual situations. Rather, the purpose of this section is to tell you steps to take to minimize your exposure to discrimination.

The key is to provide the employee with a clear explanation for letting her go. Three documents are particularly helpful in this process. If you rely on these documents when you let someone go, it is less likely that you will be charged with discrimination. The three documents are the caller rankings, the caller evaluations, and the personnel policies.

1. Caller rankings. As we will discuss later, each week you will rank your callers based on a number of criteria: dollars raised per calling session, average pledge, and pledge rate. These data are important in deciding who to let go. It provides you with objective data about a caller's job performance. Let callers go who consistently do poorly in the rankings. Discuss their ranking with them before you let them go so they understand how their performance relates to that of the other callers.

2. Caller evaluations. These evaluations, done in conjunction with monitoring, are more subjective than are caller rankings because they do not present statistical data but rather subjective comments. Nonetheless, they are valuable because they explain why a caller ranks as high or as low as he does. The caller evaluations corroborate the caller rankings, and vice versa.

As you will recall, poor callers are required to sign the caller evaluation. When you let them go, you have strong documentation that they were aware that their performance was unsatisfactory.

3. Personnel policies. To demonstrate the disparity between your expectations and their job performance, refer to the personnel policies when you fire someone. (Personnel policies are discussed in the following section.)

To:

From:

Date:

Re: Job performance

        This notice is to officially communicate to you that your
job performance is unsatisfactory. The following problems exist:

1.   Your average pledge is   . The average pledge
        for the program is   .

2.   Your dollars raised per session are   . The dollars
        raised per session per caller are   .

3.   Your pledge rate is   . The average pledge rate per
        caller is   .

Comments: _____

_____

_____

        If you have any questions, please feel free to discuss them
with me. I hope that we can work on the weaknesses identified
above. However, if there is no improvement, your employment with
(name of organization) will be terminated.

If, based on an examination of your objective and subjective evaluations of a caller, you believe the caller should be let go, give her written notice unless she is an exceptionally weak new caller, in which case let her go immediately. A sample notice appears on page 100.

The notice will serve two purposes. First, it may prompt the caller to resign, which is all the better because it saves you the aggravation of firing her. Second, it will reinforce the disparity between her performance and your expectations.

On page 102 is an example of a completed notice to a caller that her job performance is unsatisfactory. Note that the director indicated under "Comments" what period of time these statistics applied to. The statistics come from the caller records and program progress reports which are discussed in Chapter 4 in the section on record keeping.

Misconduct

Most people will be let go for poor performance. Now and then, you will have to let someone go for misconduct. A variety of behaviors are unacceptable and should result in termination.

1. Unexcused absence or lateness should not be tolerated. Your personnel policies should expressly state this.
2. Fraudulent conduct—falsifying pledges, for example—also should not be tolerated. Rid yourself of unethical callers immediately. Dishonesty is contagious. Keep in mind that bonus money is at stake, and where money is at stake, temptation is at hand. Nothing will shatter your callers' morale more completely than the lurking suspicion that the people who get the bonus money time after time are cheating. Once again, your personnel policies must make clear that fradulent conduct will not be tolerated.
3. Finally, unauthorized use of the telephone—an obvious temptation—should not be tolerated. Your personnel policies should state that no personal calls, long distance or local, are to be made without permission from the director.

Where and When to Fire

When you fire someone, do it in your office. That way you will not disturb the other callers. Do it as close to the end of the calling session as possible. That way you will not have a disgruntled person distracting the other callers.

To: S. O'HARA

From: R. BUTLER

Date: JANUARY 27, 1987

Re: Job performance

This notice is to officially communicate to you that your job performance is unsatisfactory. The following problems exist:

1. Your average pledge is $31.12. The average pledge for the program is $51.69

2. Your dollars raised per session are $190. The dollars raised per session per caller are $410.

3. Your pledge rate is 20%. The average pledge rate per caller is 32%

Comments: JANUARY 1987 STATISTICS

_____

_____

If you have any questions, please feel free to discuss them with me. I hope that we can work on the weaknesses identified above. However, if there is no improvement, your employment with (name of organization) will be terminated.

Volunteers

The key to avoiding hurt feelings when a volunteer does not make the grade as a caller is this: come up with useful alternatives for him. As you will learn later, you will always have a worthwhile position to offer a disappointed would-be caller, because a myriad of other tasks (primarily clerical) are necessary if telephone fund raising is to function well. For example, a national organization that records textbooks for the blind and relies on volunteers to make the recordings frequently has to mollify volunteers who do not qualify. "Never mind," they are told. "We also need good proofers who will make sure there are no mistakes on the recordings." Because it is clear that this role is essential, few volunteers complain about giving up the glamorous task of recording for the prosaic one of proofing.

This same tactic will work when you have a volunteer who is wasting potential contributors. Do not get rid of her. Instead, present her with alternative positions and point out that she is sure to excel in one of them. You can do this more than once with the same volunteer, treating her patiently until she finds her niche.

Use this dialogue as a rough guide:

DIRECTOR: Emma, you know it is a real joy to have you around. You are one of the most pleasant people in this calling room. But I'm afraid that we are going to have to discuss something not so pleasant. We talked about the size of your average pledge and your pledge rate last week, as I'm sure you'll recall. Neither came up to the average of the group. I've come to the conclusion that you are just too easy-going for this work. The people who do it best are the people who are not afraid to be demanding. That's not you. You are a real sweetheart, always polite.

VOLUNTEER: Well, I don't want to be rude to someone who might give us money.

DIRECTOR: That's right. But, there is a vast difference between being rude and being a tough negotiator.

VOLUNTEER (sniffling): So you don't want me to come in anymore . . . .

DIRECTOR: I very much want you to come in. I need someone with your sunny disposition and punctual nature to come in two mornings a week to help send out pledge validations. Emma, we could get $5,000 in pledges tonight, but unless the validations go out tomorrow, some of that money may never be mailed to us. That's why sending out the pledge validation is just as essential as getting the pledge. I think you'll be terrific at it. How about it? Will you try it?

VOLUNTEER: But the two evenings a week Joan and I come here are our little vacations, our evenings out of the house. She'll still be here making calls, but I won't.

DIRECTOR: Just think, Emma, you'll have two more evenings a week to relax with your husband. He'll be glad about that. You'll enjoy the morning group of volunteers. Do give it a try. Connie D'Andrea comes in then. I think you know Connie. Her Bryan is the same age as your Bruce. While the little ones are in kindergarten, the moms will be here. So, is it okay? Can I expect you Wednesday at, say, 9:30?

VOLUNTEER: Okay. Maybe Connie and I can car pool.

Notice that the director makes it her business to learn enough about her volunteers so that she can converse with them easily and persuasively. The director obviously thinks of Emma as a friend, not as just someone who comes in to work.

Personnel Policies

You will be hiring and firing a good many callers. The more callers that you deal with, the more important it is to have personnel policies that are clearly written and effectively communicated. They will establish your expectations and protect you against false allegations of discrimination or favoritism. Give each caller a copy of the personnel policies at the end of training and discuss them in the manner suggested in the section on training. Post them conspicuously in the calling room, as well. That way no one can deny knowledge of their contents.

If your personnel policies are to have meaning, they must be followed of course. So when you prepare them, make sure you can live with them; do not go overboard with too many immutable policies.

Your personnel policies should give guidelines for:

1. Calling hours.
2. Day calls.
3. Time commitment expected from each caller.
4. Starting salary.
5. Bonus structure.
6. Monitoring.
7. Raises.
8. Unexcused lateness or absence.
9. Termination of employment.

For an example, see page 105.

As you can see, the personnel policies provide guidelines. They do not always set firm rules. If you set firm rules—for example, if you state precisely how many unexcused absences will result in termination or

Personnel Policies

1. Calling hours
   Monday–Thursday, 6 PM–10 PM. Hours may be revised to meet program needs.

2. Day calls
   As needed, Monday–Friday, 9:30 AM–12:30 PM and 1:30 PM–4:30 PM. Only callers who have demonstrated strong negotiating skills at night will be eligible to make day calls.

3. Time commitment
   All callers will be expected to work at least two nights a week but no more than three. In most cases, we will be able to honor your preferences as to which nights.

4. Starting salary
   $4.50 per hour.

5. Bonus structure
   To encourage excellence, we offer the following incentives:
   • For every pledge $200 or over, you will receive a $1 bonus for each $100 pledged. For example, you will get a $3 bonus for a $300 pledge. You will get a $4 bonus for a $400 pledge. These bonuses are paid as soon as the pledge is paid or in the case of installment pledges upon receipt of the first installment payment.
   • Every evening, the callers who raise the most money will receive bonus money: first place, $6; second place, $4; and third place, $3. Conditions may be imposed; for example, a minimum average pledge of $40 may be necessary to qualify for bonus money.
   • Additional incentives may be offered as needed.

6. Monitoring
   All callers will be monitored, especially at the beginning. The purpose of monitoring calls is to diagnose negotiating weaknesses so that appropriate recommendations for improvement can be made.

7. Raises
   Excellence is rewarded. The better the caller, the more money she will earn. Raises will be given in 50¢ per hour increments. They will be determined in accordance with the caller rankings and the caller evaluations.

8. Unexcused lateness or absence
   Callers who are consistently tardy or absent will be let go.

9. Termination of employment
   • Fund raising is not for everyone. Although callers are selected carefully, sometimes we make a mistake. Often this mistake will become apparent early on, after the first calling session, for example. While we do not expect stellar results the first evening of calling, we do expect to see potential. If there is no potential for improvement, the caller's employment will be terminated.
   • Every week, your performance will be reviewed based on caller rankings and caller evaluations. Consistently poor performance will result in termination.
   • Falsification of pledges, unauthorized use of the telephone, and disruptive behavior will not be tolerated. Any caller who engages in such behavior will be dismissed.

what the minimum acceptable average pledge must be—then you must adhere to them. Otherwise, you run the risk of being charged with discriminatory application of the rules. Personnel policies should help you, not hinder you. Do not make them so specific that they deprive you of the flexibility that you need to run a successful telephone fund-raising program. The callers themselves will feel more comfortable and work better if they are guided by fair personnel policies. The opposite will be true if your personnel policies are considered to be rigid and repressive.

Adjust your policies as your particular program develops. If you change a policy or add one, give every caller a copy of the revised personnel policies. Go over the change with the callers. They must understand any change in policy so your expectations and theirs are consistent.

3

CONTACTING POTENTIAL CONTRIBUTORS

THE MECHANICS

Developing a Targeted List
of Potential Contributors

It is vital that you call people who may be in sympathy with you and not squander your resources on those who will not be. The following 15 suggestions will help you develop a targeted list, yet one that is broad enough in scope to give you the quantity of potential contributors that you need. The size and prosperity of your program hinges directly on how many good potential contributors you can locate.

1. Call your current contributors; that is, anyone who has responded to your most recent pledge request or who has contributed money on her own initiative within the last year. You can call current contributors six months after they last gave. Explain to them that it is a new fiscal year or a new tax year or that an urgent need has come up. (Tell them about the urgent need, of course.) Do not call before six months has elapsed. The risk of antagonizing the potential contributor is too great.

2. Call your former contributors; that is, anyone who supported you in the past but who did not respond to recent pledge request(s). By speaking with them, you can find out why they have not given recently, deal with their concerns, if any, and negotiate a recommitment to your cause. Telephone fund raising is the best way to turn former contributors into generous current contributors.

3. Call area businesses during the day. Choose selectively from the

Yellow Pages of the phone book, from the Business to Business Yellow Pages directory (available at most libraries), and from a list of members of the local Chamber of Commerce and from similar sources. (You will learn how to make day calls on pages 116 through 124.)

4. Swap membership lists with other organizations whose members are likely to believe in your cause. For example, if you are a group advocating reproductive rights, swap lists with a group advocating equal rights for women. Or, if you are a small theater group, swap lists with a ballet company in similar circumstances. Swap with as many appropriate groups as you can find and, ultimately, develop a network.

Networking is particularly valuable to those doing political telephone fund raising. Forming alliances with organizations that are on your side, even if only on one issue, is essential. These organizations have lists of contributors who most likely will give to your cause as well.

How do you find organizations compatible with your own? Begin by isolating the issues on which your candidate receives solid support. For example, if your candidate takes a strong stand on issues affecting farmers, contact organizations that promote those same issues. Ask them for lists of their contributors. Offer to trade names of your supporters for an equal number of theirs. If you cannot get the lists free, you may decide to buy them. But let these groups know that if they give you their lists, their interests will be served, because if your candidate succeeds, their priorities will receive attention.

In addition to working with organizations, try to acquire lists of contributors to the past campaigns of other candidates. To decide which lists to aim for, determine where your candidate falls on the political spectrum. For example, if your candidate is a moderate, try to acquire lists from conservative Democrats as well as from liberal Republicans, using the same "it's in your best interest" strategy discussed before.

If you are working for a cause rather than for a candidate, use essentially the same techniques, trying to acquire lists from candidates and organizations sympathetic to your cause. For example, if you are concerned about the environment, contact horticultural groups, anti-nuclear groups, nature study groups, hiking clubs, and the like.

5. See if your Board members and your volunteers can come up with the names, addresses, and phone numbers of members of the organizations to which they belong. They may be able to deliver to you the membership lists most organizations supply to their members.

6. Your callers acquire a list of potential contributors with nearly every call. (Each potential contributor who pledges is asked to give the names of friends who might support the cause.) Naturally, these new people should be asked to give still more names.

7. At every event you sponsor, even the strictly social, ask people to leave their names, addresses, and phone numbers on a special list. If they come to your events, they approve of your cause and probably will give generously.

8. Also call people who express interest in other ways (by writing to you, phoning, and the like). Keep a log of their names, addresses, and phone numbers.

9. Wherever crowds gather—malls, airports, train stations, fairs, rallies, celebrations—set up a table where people can pick up free pamphlets and ask questions about your organization. Keep a log handy, and encourage people to give you their names, addresses, and phone numbers.

10. Sift through the local newspaper for names of people likely to support your cause. For example, if you are a chamber music group, look for the names of attendees at musical events.

11. Enlist your local, state, and federal representatives in the cause. Their endorsement might enable you to procure lists otherwise hard to get. In addition, they might suggest unique sources of names of potential contributors.

12. There are publications that contain lists of all the members of a particular profession. For example, the *Martindale–Hubbel Law Directory* contains the names of all the lawyers in the United States and Canada and the *National Faculty Directory* contains the names of the university and college professors in the United States. If a particular occupational group is likely to support your cause, try to find the appropriate publication at the library. If that fails, try a local association connected with that particular group. For example, contact the local American Medical Association if you are looking for a list of doctors' names.

13. Contact appropriate special interest publications. They often sell lists of their subscribers' names for purposes such as yours.

14. Buy lists of names. These lists include addresses, of course. Some come with phone numbers and some without. If the list you want comes with phone numbers, so much the better. Those with phone numbers cost only slightly more, and, if you do not have the phone numbers, you will have to find them. Finding them will cost you time, money, and aggravation.

You can buy the lists from a list broker. A list broker is someone whose job it is to help you find a list that is just right for you. Before you call one, brainstorm with colleagues to draw up a profile of your perfect potential contributor. This is the first thing the list broker will ask for when you call. Let's say your organization offers free seminars to teach people how to build solar collectors to heat their hot water. Is your perfect potential contributor a bearded environmentalist with a wood-burning stove and a house surrounded by trees and full of children? Or is he a high-tech enthusiast?

Get together answers to these questions:

- Does your perfect potential contributor own his own home?
- Does he live in a single family or multifamily dwelling?
- What is his occupation?
- How much does he earn?
- How old is he?
- Is he the male head of the household?
- Is he the single head of the household?
- How many children does he have?
- How old are his children?
- Do you want to include his title, if any, in the address?

Get together answers to the following questions as well and to any other pertinent questions you can think of:

- Will you be calling companies, professionals, individuals, or all three?
- What part of the country will you be calling? (You can be as specific as zip codes.)

Focusing hard this way on what kind of constituency you want to nurture will not only help you with the list broker, but it also will help you locate good potential contributors whatever the source. For example, this information will help you decide which groups to network with. Your next step is to find a good list broker.

The library should have a set of *Standard Rate and Data* published by the Standard Rate and Data Service, Inc. When you locate these volumes, select the one called *Direct Mail Lists, Rates and Data* and within that volume look under "Mailing Lists, Brokers, Compilers and Managers." (If your library does not have this publication, contact the Standard Rate and Data Service directly at 3004 Glenview Road, Wilmette, Illinois 60091; 312-256-6067.)

List brokers advertise frequently in fund raising magazines. For example, in just one issue of *Fund Raising Management*, more than a dozen list brokers took out full-page advertisements. So when looking for a list broker, keep in mind fund raising magazines such as *Fund Raising Management* (224 7th Street, Garden City, New York 11530; (516-746-6700)

If a broker does not have the lists you seek, ask him to direct you to another broker who specializes. Finding good lists of new potential contributors becomes harder every year because you do not want to buy lists of the same people you called before. But your lists of current and former contributors will grow apace, and these lists are always winners.

Warning: sometimes callers will suggest that they call their friends. Do not let them. Insist that they stick to the potential contributor records. Hardly anyone negotiates strenuously enough with people he knows well. He counts on good will, not good negotiating, to get a nice-sized pledge, but it rarely works that way. (Remind callers that their friends may retaliate by asking for a like sum for their own favorite group.)

How to Eliminate Duplicates

With names coming in from diverse sources, you will get duplicates. Be especially aware of this if your Board members come through with lists. They probably will contain many duplicates—names of prominent potential contributors affiliated with any number of popular organizations around town.

One of the useful chores a full-service printer will do for you is the merge/purge; that is, he will combine all your lists into one workable list with as few duplicates as possible. (What else a full-service printer does and why you need one are discussed later.) If you are using several lists, you must have a merge/purge done. Do not ignore this step. A list full of duplicates is a dangerous list. Potential contributors may cheerfully accept being called once, but their mood will change rapidly with each repeat phone call.

On the other hand, eliminating every duplicate is not possible. This is especially true of married professional women. For example, Yolanda Sisneros, MD at Rittenhouse Square Professional Building also might be on your list as part of a couple, Mr. and Mrs. Charles Budd at 1227 Dundee Drive. Assuage potential contributors who complain about receiving more than one phone call by explaining that no matter how hard you try, it is impossible to eliminate all duplicates. Apologize briefly and sincerely, and move as quickly as possible back into negotiations.

Matching Callers with Potential Contributors

Patterns of giving emerge early on. For example, you may discover that potential contributors from list A are extremely generous, while those from list B are not.

Do not make the mistake of matching potential contributors with callers of commensurate excellence. The label you attach to a particular group of potential contributors or to a caller may determine how each produces. For example, if you label a caller as average and assign him only average potential contributors, you virtually insure that he remains average, despite the fact that he may have promise. Likewise, if you label a particular area as mediocre and assign only mediocre callers to that area, chances are that it will produce mediocre results, despite the fact that it may have promise. In Chapter 4, in the section on record keeping, we tell you how to determine which callers as well as which groups of potential contributors are excellent, which are good and which are average.

There are two exceptions to this prohibition. First, major donors should not be called by new callers or by average callers. They should be called by experienced callers who have demonstrated their excellence over a long time. You have too much money to lose to permit anything else.

Let your callers know in advance that only top callers will contact major donors. This will provide all the callers with an incentive to perform well. Second, this will protect directors from accusations of partiality. Callers cannot claim that favorite callers are receiving the most promising potential contributors records if they know in advance the criteria for assignment.

Second, if a caller shares a common attribute with a group of potential contributors that will make her a more effective negotiator, she should call potential contributors from that group. Let's say you are in the middle of a political campaign. Your candidate is popular with feminists. Ask a feminist to call the potential contributors whose names you acquired from a feminist organization. Or, let's say you are a university. Ask graduates of each school to call alumni from their school. Law graduates would call law alumni, dental graduates would call dental alumni, and so on. If this pairing does not produce superior results, discontinue it.

Some organizations believe that negotiations will be more productive if women call only men and men call only women. This implicitly encourages the use of sexuality to get large pledges. And, as you already know, our society has never looked upon sex in return for money with respect. Besides, the assumption that negotiations between a man and a woman are the most fruitful simply is not true. Therefore, do not make the mistake of assigning potential contributors by gender.

The Calling Room

Setting up the calling room is no easy task. You probably will be committing your program to a major expense before you have raised so much as a dollar.

Try to persuade your organization or a local business to let you use its office space and phones, if they are adequate. If this fails, use the grapevine, place an advertisement in the paper, or consult a realtor to find space from which to phone. If your telephone fund-raising is a one-shot deal, try especially hard to find donated space and phones. This is where your Board members will come in handy. Ask them to take care of this.

Consider the following when choosing a place to set up the phone room:

1. Callers need space. They also need to feel they are a part of a team. Find a room big enough to give them space and small enough to give them a feeling of intimacy.
2. You need space. Your office may have to serve as a place where small groups of callers can go for coaching. It certainly will serve as a private place where individual callers can be monitored, coached, talked to one-on-one, or fired with dignity.
3. Pledge collectors need space. As you will learn, pledge collection is an integral part of your program, and the telephone is an integral part of pledge collection. Preferably this space should be in an out-of-the way corner or in a separate but adjoining room for reasons you soon shall learn.
4. Your clerical workers need space. They need room for their tools of the trade: files, desks, typewriters, and so on.
5. You also need space in which to train callers.

Planning the Calling Room's Layout

Design the room on paper first, experimenting with various schemes. Remember to leave room for the supervisor to walk around without squeezing by and distracting the callers, who might be in the middle of tense negotiations.

You can make the room functional inexpensively with tables made out of second-quality unfinished doors and screw-on legs from the hardware store. (Tables like this are easy to dismantle and store if your program becomes temporarily smaller.) Partitioning the tables helps callers concentrate. Four callers can sit comfortably at a long table made from a door. You might be tempted to seat five or six there, but elbow-to-elbow calling leads to distractions. If you have to do without partitioned tables, the phones themselves will need to be placed further apart. Get as much free planning advice from the phone company as you can.

You will need one or two chalkboards in the calling room so you can post information that will stimulate the callers. Carefully decide where these chalkboards will do the most good. No one should have to crane his neck to check the board.

Preferably, the room will be carpeted: a carpeted room is quieter. But all those people sitting in one room also will muffle noise, so do not worry if you cannot locate a calling room with sound-deadening carpet.

If you can provide soup packets, instant coffee, cocoa, tea bags, candy, or fruit, so much the better. It may be vital for callers hurrying there from their daytime jobs, and it will be pleasant for everyone. Remember, contented callers are better callers. Just make sure they do not munch or sip while they talk on the phone.

The calling room should be a cheerful place, not a drab one. Most callers come in after already working a full day. They need visual stimulation. If the calling room is dreary, make posters out of magazines and colored papers, utilizing skills possibly untapped since kindergarten. For example, to counter a common excuse by older potential contributors that they are on fixed incomes and cannot give anything substantial, an innovative director posted a picture of the Reagans with the caption: "Not All Senior Citizens Are in the Low Income Bracket!" It did its work for a week or so and then was replaced by a poster touting credit card pledges.

Do not let the same posters, slogans, and general information stay on the walls too long or they will be neither stimulating nor informative, merely boring. One exception to this is the list of personnel policies, which should remain posted in a highly visible place, even if no one looks at it regularly. At least you made it available to the callers. If they do not study it, that is their own doing.

Why Not Just Let Everyone Call from Home?

Negotiating large pledges over the phone is not a cottage industry. You will be throwing money away if you agree to let callers take potential contributors' records home with them to call when it is convenient. Negotiating large pledges is tough, so that without competition and support from his colleagues, even the best caller does not function well.

But, like most rules, this rule is not absolute. During political campaigns, you may not have time to search for and set up a calling room. You also may not be able to persuade a local business or organization to donate phones or space, since most likely your need for a place where you can do virtually nonstop calling will exceed their generosity. Accordingly, you may have to let your callers call from home.

Just as the public vacillates about candidates and issues, so may your volunteers, consciously or subconsciously. That is why you will need to talk with them every day. That way, if you discover that a volunteer has lost heart, you can replace him immediately. Ask the volunteers to call you daily to report on their results. Let them know you need to speak with them not only to keep track of their progress, but also to gauge the political climate and to convey tips and encouragement.

The Calling Hours

Keep the calling hours flexible. Try Monday through Thursday from six to ten. Try day calls as well. (Because day calls differ substantially from evening calls, the next section is devoted to them.) And try calls during the weekends. Sunday afternoon and night, especially during the winter, are good times to call. Rarely should you call anyone on Friday or Saturday night, except possibly in the last days of a hard-fought political campaign.

If you find that a four-hour stint from six to ten is stretching it too far—catching people still enjoying their dessert or interrupting people while they are brushing their teeth at bedtime—adjust the schedule until you find what is just right. But only make an adjustment after you see a trend.

Few things are as frustrating for callers as beginning a session with a series of no contacts. To avoid this, callers should pay close attention to where they are calling and what people's schedules are in that particular neighborhood. For example, apartment dwellers in the heart of downtown may habitually stop somewhere for dinner instead of coming home to fix their own. Callers will waste time calling them before 7:30. But, out in the suburbs, Dad and Mom may get home as early as 5:30, and can be called productively at 6:00

Just as callers keep alert to differences in the schedules of city dwellers and suburban folks, they should keep alert to religious and ethnic holidays and how they affect the mood of the people to be called. Not everyone with a Jewish surname observes Passover, for example, but it is still a good idea to wait until another day to call those people. After all, potential contributors should be called at a time when they can concentrate on what callers have to say.

Do not forget your organization's own special days, and call around those times. Make special appeals at the end of your fiscal year, for example. Or anytime legislation is coming up that affects you. Or when the headlines reflect a concern of yours. If your cause is receiving publicity, make the most of it and call your supporters when they have you on their minds. That is when they can see most clearly that their contribution makes things happen.

Your calling hours may vary with the seasons. For example, if the summer months are slow, you may want to shorten your calling hours. On the other hand, November and especially December probably will be boom months, both for getting new pledges and collecting delinquent ones because potential contributors are thinking taxes then. You may want to extend your calling hours.

If your telephone fund-raising program is a one-shot deal, consider calling in shifts: from 9 AM to 12 PM, from 1 PM to 4 PM, and from 6:30 PM to 10 PM, for example. This way you make maximum use of the phones and take full advantage of the publicity you gave your program.

Finally, a note on callers' breaks. Let them take breaks at random. A uniform time for breaks does not work well because callers peak at different times. In addition, they should feel free to take a break after a trying conversation. If you have set up the bonus structure well, overlong or too-frequent breaks will not be much of a problem. Callers will be anxious to get back to the phones.

Day Calls

Where Day Calls Come From

As your callers make night calls, day calls will surface. You will probably find yourself with a stack of them before you know it. The term "day calls" denotes potential contributors who cannot be reached at night. For example, a husband may tell a caller asking for his wife that she should be called at her office during the day. Or, a potential contributor's address may obviously be a place of business. Both of these people become "day calls."

If your list is loaded with physicians, doctors, dentists, and other medical professionals, expect to find a good many day calls. Difficult as it is to reach medical professionals during the day, reaching them at home at night is next to impossible. They almost all seek the solace of an unlisted home phone number.

How to Monitor and Supervise during the Day

1. Normally, your day callers will be self-starters who can work with little supervision. They should be people who already know the

answers. You will have things to do during the day other than monitor and supervise. That is when you will be interviewing aspiring callers, seeing that pledge confirmations and reminders go out on schedule, compiling and evaluating statistics about each caller's productivity, tracking the results of your program, and the like.

2. If a number of day calls surface right away and none of your newly hired callers has become a pledge-getting luminary yet or if your best callers are otherwise occupied during the day, you will have no choice but to use callers who are good but not great. You therefore will need to monitor and coach just as you do at night.

How Long Day-Calling Sessions Should Last

Do not let people sit at the phones from nine to five. That is much too long, even if they take frequent breaks. Calling from 9:30 AM to 12:30 PM or from 1:30 PM to 4:30 PM is sufficient. Negotiating techniques deaden after a few hours.

How Many Day Callers Will Be Needed

Sometimes, during college vacations, for example, more people than you need will volunteer to become day callers. It will be tempting to take the easy way out and let them call, especially if they are loyal, productive night callers. After all, the phones are sitting idle during the day. But make sure you have enough day calls to keep callers busy. If you do not, they may gossip with one another and with your clerical staff. You will have little time to supervise or monitor dilettantish day callers.

How Many Contacts Day Callers Should Make

Day callers will not make as many direct contacts as night callers, even if they are extra diligent and make more calls per hour. It is more difficult to reach executives, physicians, and other professionals—the people who make up the bulk of the day calls—than it is to reach potential contributors at home at night. The callers' unavailability makes the problem worse. An executive or physician, for example, cannot return the call because he almost always will get a busy signal. It will be common for day callers to call executives, physicians, and other professionals a second time after making an initial contact with a secretary or office manager and ideally setting a definite time for the call back.

Remind day callers, just as you do night callers, that there is a vast difference between calling back to reach an elusive potential contributor with whom one has not yet spoken and a call back to a recalcitrant potential contributor with whom one has already negotiated. The first is necessary; the latter, unproductive.

How to Structure Bonuses for Day Callers

The hourly wage for day callers will be the same as that of night callers. But because day callers will be getting fewer small pledges and more large ones, the bonus structure should differ:

1. Daytime bonuses for first, second, and third place should not be awarded because the number of day callers will be small. Comradery, not competitiveness, motivates day callers.
2. Ample bonuses should be awarded for large pledges because day-call negotiations are demanding. If your usual bonus structure is $2 for a $200 pledge, $3 for a $300 pledge, and so on, consider giving $2.50 for a $200 pledge, $3 for a $250 pledge, $5 for a $300 pledge, $10 for a $500 pledge, and so on.
3. If you are having difficulty getting people to come in during the day, attract them by awarding a further bonus. Tie it in with the night bonus for the total number of dollars raised. Let's say the three top callers on Monday night brought in pledges totaling $750, $600, and $530. Monday morning a caller brought in pledges totaling $700. Award her a special $5 bonus just as you would if she were in second place at night. This bonus is in addition to the bonuses awarded the three top night callers. If a day caller comes in at night, too, she will begin that night session at zero dollars the same as everyone else, of course.

How to Prepare Callers to Make Day Calls

You will not need to conduct a separate training for day callers. However, you will need to meet with day callers before they begin to discuss the special problems they will encounter, problems that are gone over in detail later in this section. As you do during training sessions, blend theory with practice, and go heavy on the practice. Side by side with the discussion of these special problems, therefore, will be role play. You will play the role of a secretary, the trusted colleague of a business owner, and a time-short executive, while the callers practice dealing with each of these people.

How to Be a Successful Day Caller

The major difference between day calls and evening calls, of course, is who you will be calling. During the day, you will be calling primarily businesses, broadly defined to include doctors, lawyers, executives, and the like. Although the basic negotiating techniques remain constant, day calls require special finesse. The following five sections provide the information you need to be a successful day caller.

Who to Ask for When You Call a Business

When in doubt about whom to speak with, ask for the president of the company, or when you call non-profit-making organizations, for the executive director. Rarely will you be in doubt, of course, because you will have the name of the potential contributor in front of you on the potential contributor record. But there may be times when that person is no longer with the company or has had a change of responsibilities and you need to do some quick detective work.

Do not make the mistake of asking for Mr. Simon if the company name is, for example, E. K. Simon & Co. Mr. Simon may have nothing to do with it anymore and asking for him will identify you as someone who knows nothing about the company. In addition, do not make the mistake of assuming the president or the executive director is a man.

How to Get Past a Secretary

You take your job as a fund raiser seriously. Potential contributors have office staff who take their jobs seriously, too. Part of their job may be to protect busy executives from aggressive solicitors. How do you get around these exasperating guards?

The best way to get past the secretary is to be informal, using the executive's first name as well as your own first name, something like this: "Hi, this is Craig calling. Is Max available? He's expecting my call." Of course, the potential contributor is expecting your call because he has received the postcard that told him that you will be calling. (The postcard is discussed on pages 124 through 127.)

The secretary may ask what company you are calling from and of course you will give the name of your organization. Remember to speak confidently. Do not let a hint of apology creep into your voice. You will be asking the potential contributor to share in making the quality of life better in some way, and that is nothing to apologize for.

Sometimes the secretary's response will be icy, putting you in your place: a cool, "Mr. Patterson is on the phone," for example. Tell her you will wait. If she comes back in a few minutes and tells you he is still on the phone (she may even tell you he is on a long-distance call), hang on a bit longer. You already have a time investment, and if he really is on the phone (which often is truly the case), you know at least that he is there and that he probably will get to you next.

Another typical response is, "He's in a meeting." In this case, find out when the meeting will be over (the secretary should be able to give you at least an approximate time) and call back then. Day callers need to keep close track of the time. When a secretary says, for example, that 2:00 is when Mr. Patterson will be available, call then and not at 2:20.

Create the feeling that you and the secretary are faced with the common problem of getting you through to the executive. Keep it light: "Oh, I missed him again, did I? I'm not having good luck with him. I'll tell you what. Let's set up a telephone appointment. Shall I call him this afternoon at 3:30 or would tomorrow at 10:00 be better?" (Always suggest two times.)

If she will indicate only that the person you seek is "in and out," ask if he is more reachable early in the morning at, say, 8:30 or late in the afternoon close to 5:00. If you will not be available to call him then, pass on the information to the director of your program.

When the secretary sees how persistent you are, he may become sympathetic and put you through, if only for his own sake. After all, he is the one who has to answer the phone for all your calls. Not only will the secretary become sympathetic, but so will the executive. She, too, will appreciate your persistence and accordingly will be more likely to give.

You may be rewarded with a sizeable pledge, as was one caller who initially kept missing the potential contributor. "He's in a meeting . . . he's at lunch . . . he's not at his desk . . . he's out for the day," she was told. Finally, when the two of them did speak, the executive praised her diligence. "You've worked hard, haven't you?", he said and without much persuasion came up with $1000 for the cause.

How to Get Past a Colleague

Sometimes, instead of a secretary, it will be a colleague of the potential contributor whom you need to get past. Like the secretary, the colleague may feel responsible for protecting the potential contributor.

Speaking to a colleague of the potential contributor only wastes time. He will not remember even half of what you tell him. He will not press the potential contributor vigorously for a contribution, especially if the potential contributor is his employer. And he will not be able to answer the potential contributor's objections as you would.

Therefore, explain that you have been instructed by your organization to speak only to the potential contributor (refer to the potential contributor by his first name) and that otherwise you would be pleased to give your message to the person with whom you are speaking, implying that obviously he is a person of importance within the company.

If worst comes to worst and you get stuck actually negotiating with a colleague of the potential contributor, be forewarned: if he does not want to stick his neck out, as is usually the case, he will equivocate and refuse to pledge.

A sample day call follows. As you read it, notice the problems it presents, for we shall correct them later.

CALLER: Hello, this is Luke Ortega from Hispanics in Communications. Is Geraldo there? He's expecting my call.

INDIRECT CONTACT: You say he's expecting your call? I guess he forgot to mention it to me. I'm his associate, and I'm in charge while he's away. He won't be back until Monday. May I help you?

CALLER: Yes, please tell him that I called and that I'll call him on Monday afternoon.

INDIRECT CONDUCT: Well, Monday'll be a real busy day for him. Maybe I can help you right now.

CALLER: Thanks, but since he's expecting my call, I'll just wait until next week.

INDIRECT CONTACT: You know, Geraldo travels around the state a lot, and when he does, I'm the one who keeps things going. So, to save you time, why not tell me what's on your mind? I doubt if he'll have a chance to talk with you until at least the middle of next week. And he's leaving Friday for a convention in Austin.

CALLER: You're not the person who makes the decision about company contributions, are you?

INDIRECT CONTACT: So you're looking for money! Sure, you may as well go ahead and talk to me. Geraldo and I always discuss what we want to give.

Notice that after a good start, the caller got sucked into a trap. As soon as he mentioned "contributions," he lost control. His choice now is between refusing to discuss a contribution to Hispanics in Communications with Geraldo's associate, a refusal that would not please the associate at all, or discussing a contribution without being able to finalize a pledge.

The caller would have been better off saying something like this:

CALLER: Hm-m-m . . . it sounds as if Geraldo's schedule is as busy as your own. I'd be pleased to talk with you, but I have firm instructions to talk with Geraldo himself. I'll tell you what, though. Would you let him know that I will call him at ten on Wednesday the 27th?
INDIRECT CONTACT: Well . . . all right.
CALLER: Thanks. Good-bye.

The caller had to get off the line abruptly, but at least he was still in the associate's good graces. In addition, he obtained some worthwhile information. He found out when the potential contributor will be there and when he will not be there. He even made an appointment to call him at 10 AM on Wednesday the 27th. He will carefully note that date and time on the potential contributor's record. Geraldo probably will be extremely busy on the 27th, but most executives have demanding schedules. Catch them when they are available. No matter when you call, they will have to make room in an overloaded day for you.

How to Talk with the Executive

For productive negotiating, follow these suggestions when you speak with executives:

1. The basic idea to keep in mind is that you are offering them a chance to participate in a program that will make the quality of life better in some way. It would be unfair if you were not to let them know about such an opportunity. Certainly a lively community that has its share of thriving non-profit-making organizations—sports teams, grass roots political organizations, libraries, orchestras, museums, and the like—will keep employees happy. Employees who are pleased with the community in which they work and/or live are productive employees. Executives well understand the principle of mutual self-interest, so do not be bashful about hitting hard on this point.
2. Be respectful but not overawed, no matter how powerful the person is with whom you are speaking. Because he has the money, you may see him as the one who can set the tone of, maybe even dominate, the conversation. Not so. You have something he wants: information about how he can become a person of real importance to your cause, and by so doing can improve the quality of life for himself, his family, and his community.
3. You may have to treat the secretary or the executive's staff more circumspectly than you do the executive, who probably will welcome being talked to straightforwardly with no hesitancy. Pro-

fessionals' time is valuable. They are not accustomed to wasting it. Show that you are keenly aware of this by presenting your request concisely.

4. On the other hand, do not blurt forth your message out of respect for an executive's time. This does not work any better with executives than it does with other potential contributors. You still must turn the call into a dialogue. One caution: executives are used to controlling the conversation, but this time you must be the one in control. Review the suggestions on pages 9 through 10 about how to control the conversation.

5. Executives are apt to demand, even more often than other potential contributors, "Get to the bottom line." Do not let this throw you off. Agree with the potential contributor and respond, "Good idea!" Then ask for the money.

6. Day callers, and directors, too, should make it a habit to read the business section of the paper regularly. To talk persuasively with corporate contributors it is necessary to keep informed about business trends.

7. Is it better to force the friendship by using the potential contributor's first name? Or is it better to let him know you are impressed by his position and address him formally? Whichever you feel more comfortable with is probably better for you. When in doubt, go for informality and friendliness and call him Jim, Kirby, Zoltan, or whatever.

What to Do if an Executive Hides Behind His Budget

If a company has been giving you money right along, getting a contribution should not be difficult. The company probably has budgeted for it. Your task will be to persuade the executive with whom you negotiate to give more than the budgeted amount. Be prepared to hear, "Giving you more money would mean not being able to give any money to another deserving group."

If a company has never given you anything, the executive may pull out the same answer with a twist: "Giving you money would mean not being able to give money to another group for which we have already budgeted a contribution."

The easy answer in both cases is to find out when the company will put together its next budget and negotiate with it a month or two before. But you need the money now. Convey a sense of urgency and arrive at a pledge by letting potential contributors know that because of some special circumstance (a generous grant for which you need to raise matching funds, for example), the money will go further now than later.

Budgets usually have some leeway, especially if a top executive wants it that way.

Remember, if you belittle rival organizations, it may backfire. Instead, stress the merits of your own. In particular, point out the connection between your activities and the potential contributors' self-interest.

Pry money loose by letting potential contributors know which companies already are on your list of major donors. Surely the potential contributor does not want to be the company not on your list when you make it public.

If a company has not contributed to you before, you may have to settle for a modest gift this year just to get on its list of favorite causes. As a last resort, try hard to get at least something this time around so that the next time the company puts together its budget, the name of your organization will be a familiar one.

Making an Initial Contact

Do not call cold. Potential contributors should anticipate your call. Send them a postcard announcing it.

When cash or time is short, why not dispense with this? Do not be tempted. Unless a contact precedes his call, a caller's credibility will not be solidly established and his call will be far less likely to produce a pledge.

People often are skeptical about business conducted over the phone. The linchpin of their fear is that the caller may not be who he says he is. When a potential contributor is called after receiving a postcard heralding the call, he knows the caller is indeed who he claims to be.

Use a short, clearly worded message. For example:

> How important is your right to equal representation? We'll call you next week to find out how you feel about this.
>   Floridians for Equal Representation

> Santa Fe without local theatre? Think about it. We'll call you next week to talk about your thoughts on this.
>   The Bluestone Theatre

> Kids watching eight hours of television a day: this is a frightening thought to us. Is it to you? Tell us next week when we call.
>   The Community Center for Kids

As you see, in addition to alerting the potential contributor to your impending call, the postcard raises an issue for him to think about in the meantime. Note especially that it is not a miniletter. Do not cram information onto the card. It must be readable at a glance. Because the message on your postcard will be brief and straight to the point, chances are potential contributors will remember it. By the time they are called, they will be receptive to learning more about your organization.

Some organizations send lead letters instead. The primary advantage of a lead letter is that it can provide more information than a postcard. It can tell potential contributors about your goals, programs, and needs. A postcard, because it must be easy to read, cannot address these issues in depth.

Although a lead letter can provide potential contributors with background information that a postcard cannot, it is this very capacity that argues against its use in telephone fund raising. The problems with the letter are not inherent to direct mail, which can be highly effective. Rather, the problems are a result of combining two methods of fund raising, a letter and a phone call.

A letter may detract from the importance of the call. The better the letter, the more the potential contributor thinks about your organization. The more he thinks, the more likely he is to decide before he is called if and how much he will give. On the other hand, the weaker the letter, the less likely the potential contributor is to read it, in which case the money invested in sending it goes for naught. In other words, sending a lead letter is a double-edged sword. If the letter is too good, it may supplant the call. If it is not good enough, it may be ignored. The postcard, however, will not supplant the call because, while it raises an issue, it does not give the potential contributor enough information to make a decision. Nor will the postcard be ignored because its message can be absorbed at a glance.

In addition, a letter provides potential contributors with a perfect excuse to defer negotiations. For example, a potential contributor might say she has not yet read the letter and might ask to be called back later. A postcard—with its brief, bold message—does not give potential contributors this opportunity.

Sending a lead letter is also costly, especially if you do it right by having your letters professionally printed, dated, personalized (that is, with an inside address and salutation designating a particular person), and mailed inside an impressive envelope with a typed-on address and a first-class postage stamp.

Sending a postcard, even if you have the graphics professionally designed (as you should), is far less expensive than sending a lead letter. Postage costs alone are cut approximately in half. Postcards need not be dated or even personalized. They can be metered and labeled. If designed well, postcards still look impressive.

Finally, it is not necessary that the initial contact provide the potential contributor with information. Whatever information a potential contributor needs, the caller can provide.

The following story is for you traditionalists who find it difficult to break with the past, that is, those of you who still prefer sending the lead letter. It exemplifies a calamity that has happened thousands of times.

Dylan Carr, representing an association promoting amateur athletics, called Stephen Joplin early one summer evening. A lead letter had preceded his call, but Mr. Joplin did not recall receiving it. He asked Dylan to call him back in two days to give him time to find it and read it. Dylan tried his best to convince Mr. Joplin that the lead letter was not important. He repeated exactly what the director had instructed him to say in situations like this: "Well, it wasn't that important. It simply referred to my call."

After he said these words, Dylan was sure that Mr. Joplin would agree to continue their conversation, but instead he asked, "If the letter wasn't important, why did you send it to me?"

Dylan answered, "Well, it was important in that it referred to my call, but now that I'm speaking with you, it is no longer important."

Mr. Joplin came back with, "If it simply referred to your call, why send it? I would eventually discover you were going to call, right? Are you sure the letter didn't contain other information?"

"Actually, it did," Dylan admitted. "It described our goals, our achievements, and our plans. As a matter of fact, I have a copy in front of me. Here, I'll read it to you . . . ."

But Mr. Joplin interrupted, "Well, your organization went to a lot of time and trouble to send me that letter. I'd like to see it. Call me back when I've had a chance to read it."

Dylan reluctantly agreed. Two days later, he called back, reminded Mr. Joplin about his earlier call, and asked him if he had a chance to read the letter. Mr. Joplin said, "No, I guess it was mislaid. Please mail me another one."

Once again, Dylan pleaded with Mr. Joplin to talk with him then. But the letter by now had acquired undue importance and Mr. Joplin insisted on seeing it. So a second letter was mailed. Dylan waited five days and then called Mr. Joplin, who was away on business for two weeks. So two more weeks passed. Dylan tried Mr. Joplin again. He asked him whether he had received the letter. Mr. Joplin answered, "I don't know. In the past couple of weeks, I have received at least two dozen letters requesting money: from my church, my college, my fraternity, from people running for office, and so on and so on and so on."

"Would you please refresh my memory about the letter's contents?" he asked.

Dylan summarized the letter—almost a month after his initial call. The story isn't completely disheartening, however. After he and Dylan had talked, Mr. Joplin contributed $150 to promote amateur athletics in his town. The point is, he gave that $150 without ever reading the letter. All the letter did was delay his contribution by a month and waste precious calling time. The moral is this: if you have money, time, and energy to spare, send a lead letter. It eats up all three. If not, opt for the postcard. It is economical and effective. No potential contributor ever put off a caller by saying, "Call me back after I've read the postcard."

We assume you traditionalists are convinced. If you go ahead and use a lead letter anyway, in two months take a poll of how many people actually read it. When you discover that their number is less than 15% of those who were sent it, you will switch to the postcard.

Sending Out the Postcards

After you compose the message and have the graphics designed, you must find a good letter shop. Despite the name, letter shops also deal with postcards.

How to Choose a Letter Shop

Look in the Business to Business Yellow Pages telephone directory (your local library has one) under the categories "Letter Shop" and "Printers-Commercial." In addition, look for advertisements in local business-oriented publications. You probably will be required to pay a set-up charge as well as other one-time charges and may even be required to sign a contract, so spend some time finding the right letter shop for you considering range of services, price, and reliability. Ask for references and check them out. Sometimes new businesses will give you a good price, as a way to get established. If you use a new business, have its representatives sign a contract that clearly states their obligations.

Look for a full-service letter shop. Full service means that computer services and printing, as well as traditional letter shop services such as affixing labels and mailing, are available. Get a detailed breakdown of the letter shop's services and what they will cost. This is the only way you can adequately compare letter shops.

Do not forget to add on the cost of paper, envelopes, and postage.

Even if you need to cut corners elsewhere, go first-class when it comes to postage. If you use anything less, you take too big a chance that the postcard will arrive after your call. But if you get a bulk-mail permit and presort the postcards by zip code, they will qualify for the first-class presort rate and you can mail them at a considerable saving. Although the post office gives no guarantee about prompt delivery except for express mail, first-class presort mail receives the same priority treatment that first-class mail does.

If your program is starting small, make it clear to the letter shop representative that your program, though small at the beginning, will expand. You may be able to negotiate a better price by doing this.

If you can locate no satisfactory full-service letter shop, you will have to divide up the work. Traditional letter shops usually can recommend places that will supplement their work, businesses with whom they regularly coordinate jobs.

Look for other options that may be useful to you. For example, a senior citizens' group in Harrisburg, Pennsylvania handles routine letter shop chores free for approved non-profit-making organizations, but it is up to their clients to drop everything off (postcards and labels, for example) and afterward, mail them. And, for another example, 100 people with cerebral palsy in Philadelphia, Pennsylvania run a letter shop that accepts smaller amounts of mail than other letter shops like to handle.

What a Full-Service Letter Shop Will Do

A full-service letter shop will computerize all your lists and then purge the duplicate names. It will keep the list up-to-date by adding information such as changes of address and phone numbers and amounts and dates of pledges. It will code the names on your list so that compiling new lists (major donors, current contributors, former contributors, and so on) from the original one will be no problem. It will "pull" names. For example, if you decide to call physicians in a special appeal, it will pull out their names, if they have been specially coded, to make a new list.

Eliminating every duplicate is impossible because potential contributors might be listed under variants of their name. As you already know, this is especially true of married professional women.

A full-service letter shop will print the potential contributor record (which is described in full in Chapter 4) and will add the names and addresses, proper coding, and other essential information. Every potential contributor record will have on it a lettered source code and a sequence number. The source code tells which category the potential contributor fits into. For example, current contributors could be designated as "CC," former contributors as "FC," and so on. You can follow this same method to code your lists. Lists from the National Science Foundation could be designated "NS," from the Agricultural Alliance "AA," and so on. The sequence number tells you the potential contributor's computer number.

A full-service letter shop will print, address or label, and stamp or meter your postcards and mail them regularly, according to the time schedule you give it.

How to Decide Which Potential Contributors to Call

The letter shop and program director share the responsibility for the mailing of the postcards. The director is responsible for telling the letter shop in writing how many postcards to mail every day and to whom to mail them, and the letter shop is responsible for carrying out those instructions and reporting back in writing.

It is not a good idea to call all your excellent potential contributors, then switch to your good potential contributors, and then switch to your average potential contributors. (Once again, in Chapter 4 in the section on record keeping, you will learn how to determine whether a group of potential contributors is excellent, good, or average.) Mix these groups. Otherwise, the amount of money your program brings in will fluctuate too much. Your goal is to bring in a reasonably constant but steadily rising amount of money month after month. There probably will be seasonal peaks as well as unavoidable valleys, but manipulate the mix of potential contributors to make the flow as even as possible.

Do not attempt to impress your Board of Directors by calling all your most promising potential contributors first. The Board may indeed be impressed. But what will it think later when your results sag because you have already called the most promising potential contributors?

How to Decide How Many Postcards to Mail Each Day

Nervous directors sometimes have nightmares in which dozens of eager callers show up and find nothing on the shelves ready to be called. This kind of director overcompensates for his phobia by having too many lead postcards mailed at one time. Obviously, then, too many potential contributors' records accumulate, ready to be called. This puts the program out of synchronization, so that potential contributors often are not called until they have forgotten all about the lead postcard. Do not negate the postcard's effectiveness this way. Instead, follow these steps to calculate with relative precision the number of lead postcards you need to have mailed.

Step One

Figure out the number of calling hours for the week. Let's say you call Monday through Wednesday from 6 PM to 10 PM and that on the average there are ten callers per session. You would have a total of 120 calling hours (10 callers × 4 hours × 3 sessions).

Step Two

Multiply the number of calling hours by the number of calls that each caller will make per hour. Expect your callers to complete about seven calls per hour. To complete seven calls per hour, they will need to make approximately 30 calls per hour. (This allows for wrong numbers, no answers, indirect contacts, busy signals, call backs, and so on.) In our example, you would multiply 120 by 30 to come up with the total number of calls to be made the following week, which, of course, is 3600.

Step Three

Subtract from the total number of calls to be made (3600) the number of potential contributor records currently on the shelves ready to be called. These are records for the potential contributors who were sent postcards at least five days earlier, but who have not yet been contacted. This will give you the number of potential contributors who must be sent postcards that week.

Pledge Collection

When a potential contributor pledges, send her a pledge validation the next day. The validation can be a form that the caller simply fills in. For example:

Thank you for your generous pledge of (amount of pledge) on (date of pledge including year). As we discussed, your pledge is due in two weeks. Thank you again for your support. Please include this validation with your check.

(signature of caller)

Or, if the pledge will be paid in installments:

Thank you for your generous pledge of (amount of pledge) on (date of pledge including year). Your pledge is to be paid (semiannually, quarterly) as we agreed. The first installment of (amount of installment payment) is due in two weeks. Thank you again for your support. Please include this validation with your check.

(signature of caller)

Of course, you also will notify potential contributors when subsequent installments come due. For example:

The second (amount) installment of the (amount) pledge you made on (date of pledge including year) is now due. Thank you in advance for your continued support. Please include this notice with your check.

Not all those who pledge pay their pledges on time. It will be necessary for you to remind some potential contributors that their pledges are overdue.

Send a written reminder if the money does not arrive within three weeks after you mail the validation or the notice that an installment payment has come due. Although you need the money, do not send the reminder any earlier than three weeks after the pledge was made. People are used to paying their bills at the end of the month. That is probably when they will pay your "bill." Subconsciously, they will treat you like a creditor. Even though they may treat you like a creditor, you cannot act like one. If you send them an immediate reminder, you will be seen as an overzealous creditor, one whom they do not have to pay.

While you do not want to respond too quickly for fear of acting like a creditor, you cannot wait forever, either. People do forget. Waiting three weeks to send a reminder is a happy medium between responding too quickly and waiting too long.

The reminder must not resemble a dunning notice. Avoid negative words that will antagonize your supporters. "Urgent," "Overdue," and "Second Notice," for example, are clearly offensive. Your survival depends, at least in part, on the goodwill of your supporters. If you treat them like debtors, their goodwill will dissipate, and so will your funds. They cannot say no to the bank or the electric company, but they can say no to you.

The reminder should do three things: (1) thank the potential contributor for her pledge; (2) let her know that you are still counting on her support; and (3) ask her to send the payment as soon as possible.

The reminder can be a form. Simply fill in the relevant information. A sample follows:

On (date of pledge including year), when our caller spoke with you, you were most generous and pledged (amount of pledge). If you have already mailed us your check, please disregard this notice and accept our heartfelt thanks. If you have yet to mail it in, please do so now. We are counting on your gift of (amount of pledge).

Your gift is important to us. This year we are relying on people like you for 70% of our budget. With declining federal support, only generous public support can guarantee that we will be open on weekends during the summer.

I hope you will mail in your check as soon as possible and that you continue to enjoy the Art Museum.

Or, if the reminder follows the notice that an installment payment was due, use the following sample:

On (date of pledge, including year), when our caller spoke with you, you were most generous and pledged (amount of pledge) to be paid (semi-annually/quarterly). The (second/third/fourth) installment of (amount of installment payment) is due. If you have already mailed us your check, please disregard this notice and accept our heartfelt thanks. If you have yet to mail it in, please do so now.

Your gift is important to us. This year we are relying on people like you for 70 percent of our budget. With declining federal support, only generous public support can guarantee that we will be open on weekends during the summer.

I hope you will mail us your check as soon as possible and that you continue to enjoy the Art Museum.

Make it as easy as possible for potential contributors to send in their pledges by including a postage-paid return envelope when you mail them the pledge validation, a notice that an installment payment is due, or a reminder that a pledge is overdue.

If the money does not arrive within three weeks after you send the reminder (a total of six weeks after the pledge was made or an installment came due), it is time to telephone the potential contributor. Because pledge collection by telephone is more personal than pledge collection by mail, it is more effective. It also is more time consuming, so send a written notice first and only call those who do not respond.

Common Problems That Pledge Collectors Encounter

1. The potential contributor cannot honor her commitment because of financial difficulties. This is the most common reason for ignoring the commitment. An unforeseen event has drained a potential contributor's bank account. Or, a potential contributor pledged, then discovered she had less readily available money than she thought. When confronted by someone like this, do not try to make her adhere to her initial pledge. She will resent that and give you nothing. Do not let her off the hook entirely, either. Renegotiate a more moderate commitment.

Renegotiation is a four-step process. First, sympathize with the potential contributor. Let him know he is not unique and that many people you speak with are in similar situations. Second, tell him that while you are sympathetic, your organization still needs help. Third, tell him that you are confident that you can restructure his pledge to take into account his changed circumstances. And, finally, propose a new amount. To demonstrate that you are responding to his particular needs, make your new request noticeably lower. Ask for approximately 70% of the original pledge. Dropping significantly less than 30% will be seen as nothing more than a gesture. Dropping significantly more than 30% will be too great a concession. If the potential contributor does not say yes, negotiate downward as you would with any potential contributor on an initial call.

The dialogue that follows illustrates the art of renegotiation.

PLEDGE COLLECTOR: Hello. This is Stephen Edelstein calling from the United Jewish Council for Laurence Gottlieb.

POTENTIAL CONTRIBUTOR: This is Larry. What can I do for you?

PLEDGE COLLECTOR: I am calling about the $150 pledge you made on December 6. Have you sent it in yet?

POTENTIAL CONTRIBUTOR: No, I'm sorry. I have not. Last week our roof began to leak. It is going to cost me at least $800 to get it fixed. I really can't afford any charitable giving right now.

PLEDGE COLLECTOR: I'm sorry to hear about your roof, Larry. I imagine that, in addition to the cost, it's a real nuisance. If it makes you feel any better, you're not the only person I have spoken with this evening who has recently been hit with an unexpected expense that prevented him from honoring his initial commitment. We are also in a squeeze. Money is tight here, and, as I'm sure you know, every pledge helps. You sound as if you would like to give. The problem is the pledge agreed upon in December is too high. Why don't we try something more moderate, something feasible in light of your changed circumstances? How about a pledge of $100? That would still go a long way toward helping us achieve our goals and, at the same time, would not be as difficult for you.

POTENTIAL CONTRIBUTOR: I appreciate what you're trying to do. I just don't have $100. If I did, I'd gladly send it to you.

PLEDGE COLLECTOR: How about $50? Is that more manageable? You can put it on your credit card. That way you can spread out the payments to suit yourself. And that pledge works out to less than $1 a week!

POTENTIAL CONTRIBUTOR: That sounds reasonable. And, yes, I'd like to use my credit card.

What was a lost pledge was turned into a $50 gift. All the written reminders in the world could not have achieved this result.

2. The potential contributor denies ever making a pledge. This indeed is a problem, especially if what the potential contributor says is true. Apologize for the mistake and quickly get off the phone. Do not try to negotiate a pledge. Your efforts will go for naught. A potential contributor who receives a reminder about a pledge she never made is not likely to support your organization immediately thereafter because the mistake often is perceived as intentional.

The following dialogue is illustrative:

PLEDGE COLLECTOR: Hello, this is Andrew Schaeffer calling from the Jefferson School for Jodi Vinnick.
POTENTIAL CONTRIBUTOR: This is Jodi. I received your pledge reminder. But I never made any pledge. As a matter of fact, I never spoke with anyone from the school.
PLEDGE COLLECTOR: I'm very sorry. Apparently we have made a clerical mistake. I'll make sure it is rectified. Have a good evening.

Of course, the caller who recorded the pledge should be spoken to immediately.

3. The potential contributor made the pledge and has the money but no longer wishes to give. Something caused the potential contributor to believe that you no longer are worthy of his support. Usually his change of heart involves a person, policy, or program, the same concerns that preclude some potential contributors from giving initially.

Respond as you would if the concern were raised in the initial call. Do three things. First, recognize its validity. Second, explain your position. Third, ask the potential contributor to honor his pledge. The following two dialogues illustrate this process:

Dialogue I

PLEDGE COLLECTOR: Hello, this is Melissa Kay calling from WCLU for David Kreichman.
POTENTIAL CONTRIBUTOR: This is David.
PLEDGE COLLECTOR: I'm calling to talk to you about the $140 pledge that you made to public radio on February 7. Have you sent in your second installment of $70?
POTENTIAL CONTRIBUTOR: No, I haven't. And I don't intend to. I read that the director of the station has a salary in excess of $50,000 per year. If you can afford to treat your executives as if they were in the private

sector, then you don't need public sector support, at least not from me.

PLEDGE COLLECTOR: I understand your feelings. I think that you have a very valid point. You're not the first person to voice that concern. Let me assure you that your comments will not go unnoticed.

POTENTIAL CONTRIBUTOR: What good will that do?

PLEDGE COLLECTOR: I can't promise anything. But, because 65% of our support comes from the public, your concerns are very important to our Board of Directors. Despite your uneasiness with Mr. Burton's salary, I'm sure you still appreciate our programming and the public service function that we perform. Also, only 15% of our revenue goes to salaries. Almost 50% goes directly to programming. How about that $70, David? Think of the programming!

Dialogue II

PLEDGE COLLECTOR: Hello, this is Scott Greenberg calling from the Fisch campaign for Gary Brooks.

POTENTIAL CONTRIBUTOR: This is Mr. Brooks.

PLEDGE COLLECTOR: I'm calling about the $50 pledge that you made on March 3, Mr. Brooks. Have you sent it in yet?

POTENTIAL CONTRIBUTOR: No, I haven't, and I don't know that I'm going to.

PLEDGE COLLECTOR: Why the change of heart?

POTENTIAL CONTRIBUTOR: I was very disappointed when Mr. Fisch did not speak out during the school board crisis. The opposition did. It's important to speak out, no matter how controversial or politically explosive the issue.

PLEDGE COLLECTOR: I understand how you feel. You have a valid point. We made a mistake. We should have responded as soon as the issue arose. We have tried to make amends. We took out a full page ad in Sunday's paper which clearly states our position. Our position, in a nut shell, is . . . .

POTENTIAL CONTRIBUTOR: I wish he had made his feelings on this issue clear earlier.

PLEDGE COLLECTOR: So do we. But there's nothing more we can do now. We hope you'll look past it and concentrate on those issues that prompted you to support us initially. Your support is very important to us. The election is less than two weeks away, and we have so much to do. To win, we need money, and that includes yours. How about it, Mr. Brooks? Can we count on you to honor your $50 pledge?

A sample pledge collection script follows. Use it as the model for your own script.

Pledge Collection Script

Introduction

Hello, this is (your name) calling from the St. Anne Day Care Center for (potential contributor's name). I would like to speak with you about the (amount) pledge that you made to the Center on (date of pledge). Have you sent it in yet? (If an installment payment is due, ask the potential contributor whether she has sent it in.)

Responses

If the Potential Contributor Says, "Yes"

Thank you very much for your support. I'm sorry to have bothered you. We must have made a clerical mistake, because I have no record of your payment. I'll make sure that it is noted.

If the Potential Contributor Says, "No, I don't Have the Money"

I can appreciate your financial situation. (Be specific, if possible.) If it makes you feel any better, you're not the only person I have spoken with this evening who has recently been hit with an unexpected expense that has prevented him/her from honoring his/her commitment.

We are also in a squeeze. Money is tight here, too. And, as I'm sure you know, every pledge helps. You sound as if you would like to give. The problem is that the pledge agreed upon on (date of pledge) is too high. Let's try something more moderate, something feasible in light of your changed circumstances. How about a pledge of (approximately 70% of the initial pledge)? That would still go a long way toward helping us achieve our goals and at the same time would be less difficult for you. (If the potential contributor says "no," negotiate downward as you would if this were the initial call. Use the negotiating chart on page 138.)

If the Potential Contributor Says, "No, I Never Made a Pledge"

I'm very sorry. Apparently we have made a clerical mistake. I'll make sure that the mistake is rectified. Have a good evening.

If the Potential Contributor Has a Particular Complaint About the Organization

(Do three things. First, recognize the validity of the potential contributor's complaint. Second, explain the organizations position (for example, describe the corrective measures that have been taken.) Third, ask the potential contributor to honor his pledge. Negotiate downward, if necessary. Use the negotiating chart on page 138.)

Validation

Thank you very much. We will expect your pledge as soon as possible, preferably within one week. Let me check your address. It is _____. The amount of your pledge is $_____. I will send you a pledge validation tomorrow and a postage-paid return envelope. Please return the validation form with your check so we can credit it properly. Thank you again for your pledge of $_____.

Follow-up

If the potential contributor agrees to honor his initial pledge or to send in a renegotiated pledge, mail him a pledge validation. Once again, this can be a form:

Thank you for agreeing to pay your (pledge/installment payment) of (amount of pledge/installment payment). Please include this validation with your check.
(caller's signature)
Date of pledge: (date including year)

Who Should Do Pledge Collection

In an ideal world, one in which you had unlimited time and money, you would hire callers specifically to do pledge collection. They would be given a separate training, they would call from a separate location, and so on. But the world is not ideal: time and money are scarce. Accordingly, use callers who are already in the calling coterie, callers already trained and familiar with your program. A good rule of thumb: you will need only one pledge collector for every five callers. (You may want to increase the number of pledge collectors in November and December because as you know these are boom months for fund raising.)

Although calling for new pledges and collecting overdue ones have many common elements, the differences between them are substantial.

Negotiating Chart

Ask for	Make it manageable	Break it down	Additional information
$150 Pledge	$75 Semiannually or $37.50 quarterly	Less than $3 a week Less than 50¢ a day (less than the cost of a cup of coffee)	We are in the process of negotiating a low-interest rate bank loan. We can only get this loan if we show the bank that we have sufficient collateral. So you see, we need your help now so we can increase the services we offer. If we can't expand now, we might never have as good a chance.
$100 Pledge	$50 Semiannually or $25 quarterly	Less than $2 a week Less than 30¢ a day (less than the cost of the daily paper)	
$75 Pledge	$37.50 Semiannually	Less than $1.50 a week Less than 25¢ a day (the cost of a phone call)	Three day care centers in our area closed last year because they didn't have the funds to stay open. Your commitment this evening not only will help insure our survival, but it also will help us grow.
$50 Pledge	$25 Semiannually	Less than $1 a week Less than 15¢ a day	
$35 Pledge		Less than 70¢ a week Less than 10¢ a day	
$25 Pledge		Less than 50¢ a week Less than 8¢ a day	

Therefore, a caller who tries to do both does neither well. Once a caller begins doing pledge collection, she should concentrate on developing those skills exclusively and should not return to the calling coterie unless she is retrained.

Do not use your best callers as pledge collectors. Their talents will not be utilized fully. Negotiating is a part of every initial call, but it is a part of only some collection calls. Instead of using good callers, use callers who are only average. They have negotiating skills that are adequate for pledge collection and, equally important, removing them from the calling coterie will not cause your fund-raising efforts to suffer. You can replace them with better callers.

In addition to knowing how to negotiate, pledge collectors must be trustworthy. You need to know why pledges are not coming in. Pledge collectors are responsible for keeping track of those pledges that potential contributors claim never were made. This responsibility puts pledge collectors in the position of implicating their colleagues in misconduct, so only choose people you can trust and make it easy for them to stay aloof from peer pressure by giving them their own separate calling area.

You need not hold a separate training for pledge collectors, but you will need to meet with them before they begin calling. Go over the pledge collection script, focusing on the special problems they will encounter as pledge collectors. Make sure they have a copy of common problems. Role play with them until they feel comfortable as pledge collectors, with you in the roles of a potential contributor with financial difficulties, a potential contributor who denies ever making a pledge, and a potential contributor who no longer wishes to honor his pledge because he has a complaint. Practice until the pledge collectors become adept at turning an overdue pledge into a renegotiated one.

While potential contributors have a moral obligation to honor their commitments, they usually are not contractually bound. Gratuitous promises, as a general rule, are not legally enforceable. Accordingly, pledge collectors should not imply that they are. Make sure they understand this.

As time allows, monitor and coach pledge collectors to make sure they are performing the renegotiating part of their job correctly.

Pay pledge collectors the same hourly rate as you do your other callers. This is necessary, even though doing pledge collection is less demanding, because pledge collectors receive no bonuses. There is no fair way to administer a bonus system for pledge collection. Pledge collectors' results are predetermined to some extent by the actions of the initial callers.

Thanking Potential Contributors

Everyone who honors his commitment should receive an acknowledgment in addition to the thanks that is expressed in the pledge validation. It is more than a simple courtesy. It is good business sense. People
are more likely to continue to give when their philanthropy is recognized. Thanking a contributor for his gift this year is actually the first
step in garnering his support next year.

Just as sending a lead postcard saves time and money, so does
sending a thank-you postcard, even if you have the graphics professionally designed, as you should. The postcard can be a form. Simply fill
in the relevant information. New contributors, former contributors, and
current contributors should receive different messages, however, as the
following examples illustrate

New Donor:
On behalf of the New Orleans Ballet, I would like to thank you for your
gift of (amount of gift). Welcome to our family of supporters. Your contribution will help insure that we continue to thrive as a New Orleans institution.
    (signature of Program Director)

Lapsed Donor:
On behalf of the New Orleans Ballet, I would like to thank you for your
gift of (amount of gift). We are happy that you are supporting us once
again. Your contribution will go a long way to help insure that we continue to thrive as a New Orleans institution.
    (signature of Program Director)

Renewed Donor:
On behalf of the New Orleans Ballet, I would like to thank you for your
gift of (amount of gift). Your consistent support has helped us remain a
New Orleans institution.
    (signature of Program Director)

It is not necessary to send potential contributors who divide their
gift into installments a thank-you postcard after each payment. Send
one only after you receive the first installment. This postcard also should
reflect the category of the potential contributor to whom it is addressed.
For example, a current contributor would receive a message like this:

On behalf of the New Orleans Ballet, I would like to thank you for your
payment of (amount of payment) toward your pledge of (amount of
pledge). Your consistent support has helped us remain a New Orleans

institution. We look forward to continued growth. And, of course, we look forward to the receipt of the remainder of your pledge when it comes due. Thanks again.
(signature of Program Director)

Major donors should be sent a special letter, not a postcard. Their substantial support justifies the additional cost. The letter should be signed by someone prominent, an eminent volunteer or the executive director of the organization, for example. The letter need not be lengthy. One paragraph will suffice. For example:

Dear Mr. Leos:
I would like to take this opportunity to thank you for your gift of $200. It is people like you who are directly responsible for making us one of the most successful private ballet companies in the country. With this kind of generous support, we can continue to present the quality productions that you have come to expect and enjoy. Once again, let me thank you on behalf of the entire company. If you have any questions, ideas, or thoughts about the New Orleans Ballet, please feel free to call and share them with us.
Sincerely,
(signature of Program Director)

Major donors, like other donors, should receive a thank-you letter only after the first installment is paid. It is not necessary (indeed, it is financially unadvisable) to thank them separately for each payment. Nor is it necessary that the thank-you letter differentiate between types of supporters. Every major donor is already in a special class. The thank-you letter, like the thank-you postcard, will be slightly different if the pledge is paid in installments. In most cases, installment pledges will be covered by letters and not postcards because installment pledges are larger than average. A sample installment thank-you letter follows:

Dear Mr. Leos:
I would like to take this opportunity to thank you for your $100 payment toward your pledge of $200. It is people like you who are directly responsible for making us one of the most successful private ballet companies in the country. With this kind of generous support, we can continue to present the quality productions that you have come to expect and enjoy. Once again, let me thank you on behalf of the entire company for your pledge of $200. If you have any questions, ideas, or thoughts about the New Orleans Ballet, please feel free to call and share them with us.
Sincerely,
(signature of Program Director)

Summary of the Process

Here, in a nutshell, is the magical nine-step process during which the names of potential contributors change from abstract harbingers of prosperity on a piece of paper into money in the bank—lots of it!

1. Gather as many names of potential contributors as you can.
2. Have the whole batch merged/purged and appropriately coded.
3. Have the potential contributor records as well as the postcards, pledge validations, installment-due notices, reminders, and thank-yous printed.
4. Have the pertinent data about the potential contributors entered onto the potential contributor records.
5. Begin the cycle: the mailing of the postcard followed by the phone call five days later.
6. After people pledge, mail them a pledge validation.
7. After people send in their money, mail them a thank-you.
8. If the money does not arrive within three weeks, send the potential contributor a reminder.
9. If three weeks later the money still has not arrived, call the potential contributor.

The Clerical Side of Pledge Collection

You will need a filing system so that you will know when to notify potential contributors that their installment payments have come due. We recommend the following system.

Step One

Make as many copies of the potential contributor record as there will be installment payments after the first payment. For example, since there are two payments in a semiannual pledge, you will need to make one copy. Likewise, since there are four payments in a quarterly pledge, you will need to make three copies.

Step Two

File a copy under each date on which an installment will fall due. Let's say that on February 18 a potential contributor pledges $400 to be paid in quarterly installments. You will need to file a copy of his record under May 18, August 18, and November 18.

Step Three

Each day mail notices to potential contributors whose records are filed under that date. For example, on October 26 you will mail notices to all potential contributors whose records are filed under October 26.

You also will need a filing system so that you will know when to collect overdue pledges; that is, when to send reminders and when to make collection phone calls. This filing system is separate from the one designed to notify potential contributors when their installment payments come due. We recommend the following system

Step One

After a pledge is made, make a copy of the potential contributor record. File the original record alphabetically by last name. File the copy under the date on which the pledge is made. For example, if Eleanor Myles pledges $250 on June 1, you would file her original potential contributor record under "M" so it can be located easily and you would file the copy of her record under "June 1."

Step Two

When a payment arrives, indicate this on both the original record and on the copy by writing "pd" and the date of receipt. Because potential contributors are asked to return their validations with their checks, when their money arrives it is easy to see under which date their record is filed. However, if, for example, Ms. Myles does not return her validation, all you need do when her check arrives is look under "M" to locate her potential contributor record. This will tell you under which date her other record is filed.

Step Three

If the potential contributor agreed to pay his pledge all at once, after payment arrives and you have indicated payment on both the original record and the copy, refile them in the same manner they were filed before (*alphabetically* as well as *by date of pledge*) in another filing system labeled "Paids." The alphabetical file tells you who your current contributors are. The chronological file tells you when you can call them for another gift. As you already know, no current contributor should be called within six months of his most recent gift.

If the potential contributor agreed to pay his pledge in installments, after his first payment arrives and payment is indicated on both the original and the copy, refile the copy under the next due date. For example, if on January 15 a potential contributor pledges $200 to be paid quarterly and his first installment payment of $50 arrives on January 26, you would refile a copy of his record under April 15 and put the original back where it was. Of course, you would repeat this procedure with each upcoming installment until his records—the original and the copy—enter the "Paids" files.

Step Four

Each day mail reminders to potential contributors whose records are still in the file dated three weeks prior to the current date. For example, on November 22 you would send reminders to potential contributors who pledged on November 1, but had yet to pay. (As you will recall, reminders are sent to potential contributors who do not pay within three weeks.)

Step Five

Each day pull the potential contributor records that are still in the file dated six weeks prior to the current date. For example, on November 22 you would pull the file dated October 11 so that your telephone pledge collectors can call those potential contributors. (As you will recall, collection phone calls are made to potential contributors who do not pay within three weeks after the reminder is sent, which is six weeks after the pledge was made.)

Two additional points: first, if payment does not arrive within two weeks of the pledge collection call, eight weeks after the pledge initially was made, it probably never will arrive. So, each day, pull the file of potential contributor records that is dated eight weeks prior to the current date. Remove the corresponding potential contributors records from the alphabetical files and put them in storage. Second, if a potential contributor denies ever making a pledge (during a pledge collection call, for example) and if the alleged pledge was to be paid in installments, make sure that you remove all copies of the potential contributor record from the installment notice file as well as from the pledge collection file so that you do not waste time and money trying to collect these uncollectable pledges.

Whether you use file drawers or computer files, the step-by-step approach that we recommend for filing pledges will work for you.

4

STRUCTURING AND ADMINISTERING YOUR TELEPHONE FUND-RAISING PROGRAM

Planning Your Program

Why Planning Is Important

Now that you know everything you need to know about negotiating large pledges, developing a coterie of top-notch callers, and contacting potential contributors, you are ready to think about starting your program. The first step is planning.

Planning is an integral part of establishing and maintaining a successful telephone fund-raising program. So, unless you have no choice but to plunge in headfirst—because you are in a close political campaign that is about to come to an end, for example—take time to plan.

Why is planning so important? By having a written plan against which to check your results, you can tell at a glance whether your program is developing consistently and producing the results that you seek.

How to Determine the Size and Length of Your Campaign

1. Set your goal. How much money do you need to raise? Let's assume your goal is $300,000.
2. Determine the number of names you need to reach that goal. To do this, divide your goal by $7.65. In our example, that would be

39,216. You would need 39,216 names to reach your $300,000 goal.

How did we come up with $7.65? The following example explains how. Let's say you have four lists with a total of 1000 names. On the average, 15% of those names will be duplicates and therefore will be eliminated in the merge/purge. This leaves you with 850 names. Of those 850 names, your callers will reach approximately 60%. The other 40% are unreachable: never home, never available, moved, deceased, and so on. This means that you will reach 510 potential contributors (0.60 × 850) or 51% of the 1000 names. Of the 510 calls completed, approximately 30% will result in a pledge. Of course, this number will vary depending on the quality of your callers and the generosity of the particular group of potential contributors who you are calling. But probably out of the 1000 names, 153 will pledge (0.30 × 510). The average pledge in your program probably will be approximately $50. Once again, this number will vary depending on the quality of your callers and who you are calling. But probably your 153 pledges will produce approximately $4650 ($50 × 153). This amounts to $7.65 for each name on your original four lists ($7650 ÷ 1000).

How long will it take you to achieve your goal?

1. Figure out the number of potential contributors you will reach (51% of the names).
2. Divide this number by seven. This will give you the number of calling hours it will take to achieve your goal. You divide by seven because, as you know, callers on the average complete seven calls per hour.
3. Divide the number of calling hours it will take to achieve your goal by the number of calling hours in your program per week, which is the number of hours per week in which calls are made multiplied by the number of callers working per hour. This will give you the number of weeks it will take to achieve your goal.

So how long will it take you to raise $300,000 with your 39,216 names?

1. You will reach 20,000 of the potential contributors (0.51 × 39,216).
2. This will take 2857 calling hours (20,000 ÷ 7).
3. Let's say that, on average, you have ten callers calling four nights a week, four hours per night. That means there are 160 calling hours per week in your program (10 × 4 × 4). Therefore it will

take you approximately 18 weeks to reach your goal (2857 ÷ 160 = 17.86).

If you want to complete the calling more quickly, you will have to increase your calling hours either by increasing the number of hours in which calls are made each week or by increasing the number of callers. Likewise, if you want to proceed more slowly, you will have shorter or fewer calling sessions or use fewer callers.

How to Extend Your Program

After you reach your goal, you may decide to extend your program. Let's say, for example, you came up with 100,000 names initially and reached 51,000 of whom 30% pledged an average pledge of $50. In other words, a total of $765,000 was pledged (51,000 × 0.30 × $50). Now, at your request, your list broker comes through with 20,000 additional names from a geographic area that was very supportive the first time around.

How much money should you expect from these people? You can come up with good projections based on your own experience. Let's say that while the average pledge overall was $50, the average pledge for this group was $70. And while the average pledge rate was 30% the pledge rate for this group was 40%. Assuming a 49% fallout (duplicates and unreachables), your callers will contact 10,200 potential contributors, which of course is 51% of 20,000. If 40% pledge, the number of contributors in the group will be 4080 (0.40 × 10,200). If the average pledge is $70, you should collect an additional $285,600 from this group.

After you begin calling, you will be able to make projections and plan ahead, just as we have done. When you begin, however, and do not have your own figures, use our estimates. To review, they are:

1. You will reach approximately 51% of the names you acquire. The other 49% are either eliminated as duplicates or unreachable.
2. Approximately 30% of all potential contributors will pledge.
3. The average pledge will be approximately $50.

Additional Decisions You Will Need to Make

Determining the size and length of your campaign is only the first step in planning. There are a number of additional decisions that need to be made. They include:

1. Do we need the approval of the Board of Directors before going ahead with this program? (The next section tells you how to gain the support of the Board of Directors.)

2. Who will our potential contributors be?
3. Where will we call from?
4. What will our calling hours be?
5. Should we offer clubs and premiums? (A later section will tell you how to arrive at this decision.)
6. Shall we use paid callers or volunteers?
7. Where will we find our callers?
8. How many callers do we need?
9. How many clerical workers will we need? (Clerical tasks are discussed later.)
10. How much money do we have with which to get started?

As you see, you already have or soon will acquire all the information you need to arrive at these decisions. The last question, how much start-up money you have, is obviously the most important. The amount of start-up money you have will affect your answers to most of the other questions.

Gaining the Support of the Board of Directors

Despite the popularity and overwhelming success of telephone fund raising among all types of organizations, you may have some trouble convincing your Board of Directors to give it a try. Telephone fund raising is an assertive art; that is why it works so well. To some Board members, however, it may seem too assertive. When asked about her feelings on telephone fund raising, one Board member said, "Calling people at home and asking them for money! We can't resort to that." Two months later, when her organization was on the verge of collapse, she relented and agreed to give telephone fund raising a try. Well, the story would not be complete if we did not tell you that the organization is thriving today, in part because of its telephone fund-raising program.

If you meet some resistance from your Board when you introduce the telephone fund-raising concept, do not be discouraged. You can sway the Board by clarifying the process. Be forthright about the hard facts about telephone fund raising, specifically its complexity and expense. The Board members may want to see it your way—after all, who can ignore the attraction of big money—but may need to be convinced, especially if your organization has a conventional fund-raising history or, worse, no fund-raising history at all. Make sure you explain—just as we explained to you—how the size of your program can be determined and, if appropriate, how the program can be expanded.

If the Board still cannot decide whether or not to go forward with telephone fund raising, convince them with a one-shot deal. In other words, with the Board's permission, focus on one specific goal: raising enough money to computerize the ticket-selling process, for example, if you are a theater. Decide how much money you need to raise, how long that will take, and go to work. Once a Board sees how astonishingly productive telephone fund raising can be, they rarely hesitate to back the program in an ongoing way.

After you have convinced the Board to give telephone fund raising a try, use the Board to help you make the program flourish. While the Board will not be involved in the day-to-day administration of your program, it can play a role. The relationship between the telephone fund-raising program and Board members should not be passive. An active Board will have a vested interest in your program and therefore will be less likely to oppose it.

Among the functions that the Board should perform are the following:

1. Board members should do their best to make the facilities and expertise of the companies where they work available to you. Of course, they cannot do this unless they know your needs. Prepare for the Board a list of things that you need: calling space and phones, for example. Distribute the list to the Board with a request for help.
2. Board members should direct you to companies where they have contacts which may, for example, let you use their word-processing equipment or computers or let you advertise for callers or clerical workers in the company newsletter or on company bulletin boards. Once again, you must let the Board members know your needs so they can help satisfy them.
3. Board members may help you add to your list of potential contributors by giving you membership lists from the organizations to which they belong. Board members tend to be joiners. They know many people and usually are affiliated with many groups. Take advantage of their contacts to develop a strong following.

Board members will expect something from you in return. Your gift to them is the money that you raise which makes their lives easier. You cannot expect them to realize this. You have to tell them.

Later, in this chapter, we discuss record keeping. As you will learn, you will keep records on your program to gauge its progress. Board members should receive copies of these reports before each Board meeting. By the way, it is good form to get this information to the Board several days before the meeting so they will have time to focus their thinking and formulate questions.

If an unusual expense occurs (for instance, if you buy several radio spots advertising for callers) or if your program is not as productive as usual one month, write up an explanation for the Board in memo form. Do not leave them without an explanation. Otherwise they will come up with one of their own, one that might affect the longevity of your program.

Likewise, if you have a banner month, note this in a memorandum. There is nothing wrong with boasting about your success. If you do not do it, no one will.

And, of course, share your plans with the Board. Showing that you intend to build toward your goals in a steady, rational way gives them credibility, no matter how high you have reached.

In sum, make sure the Board clearly understands how telephone fund raising works and how it can benefit your organization. If the Board members hesitate to endorse it, ask them if you can test telephone fund raising in a limited way with a one-shot deal. Then, take advantage of the success of the one-shot deal to get telephone fund raising established as an ongoing program. Use the Board and its contacts when you need facilities and the names of potential contributors, for example. Regularly present the Board with reports so they are never in doubt as to how the program is developing.

Public Relations

Telephone fund raising does not exist in a vacuum. You are not raising money just to raise money, but to provide your organization with the funds it needs to reach its goals. When people are well-informed about those goals, and about your organization in general, the more readily they will contribute. This is where public relations comes in: the role of public relations is to give people positive information about your organization so they will want to support it.

If your organization has a special public relations person or department, you will need to keep the public relations specialist informed about telephone fund raising milestones, so he can publicize them properly. But, in most cases, it will be up to you to handle the public relations for your program. What are the best ways to go about this?

1. Rely on the callers. Every caller is a purveyor of positive information. The callers themselves are your most effective public relations tool.

2. Use the media. You can influence great numbers of people by getting publicity in the newspapers and on radio and television. Chances are that some Board members have media contacts. Make friends with these contacts. Meet with them personally, preferably with the Board member along. Invite them to visit the calling room so you can introduce them to the callers. Offer to be a source of information about your program. Remember, however, that the media thrives on controversy and will attempt to use you just as you attempt to use it.

Even if Board members do not have media contacts, they can help you monitor the media to keep tabs on how it is presenting your point of view. If your organization or your cause is getting a good press, you may want to take advantage of it by increasing the calling hours temporarily. If you are getting a bad press, you will need to discuss this with the callers and prepare a special Common Problems sheet, perhaps supplemented by role playing, so that the callers will know how to respond when potential contributors bring up controversial issues.

3. Mail a newsletter, quarterly, or similar publication to all your contributors. It should contain solid information that potential contributors cannot easily find elsewhere. That way it becomes indispensable. For example, Network, a Catholic lobbying group, lets its contributors know how Congress voted on issues of crucial importance to them. The Union of Concerned Scientists reviews books its contributors might not otherwise hear about. The College of Letters and Science at the University of California at Berkeley lets its graduates know how their contemporaries are prospering. Of course, these organizations, like most others, also use their publications to give supporters basic information about the status of the organization—what it has done, what it is doing, what it intends to do.

4. Make your budget available. Although most potential contributors will have no interest in seeing your budget, a few will not be satisfied until they do. It is good sense, therefore, from a public relations viewpoint to make your budget available upon request. Potential contributors can clearly see for themselves, then, that they are not paying for unproductive fund-raising methods.

Clubs and Premiums

As you will recall, although clubs and premiums can be useful negotiating tools, many organizations do not use them. This is because although they can help you, they also can hurt you. You already know how they can help you (see pages 24 through 27). Here is how they can hurt you:

1. Inexperienced callers often overemphasize clubs and premiums. This is because it is easier to discuss what the potential contributor will receive than to discuss what he should give.
2. Clubs and premiums cost your organization money. Even if the benefits that accrue to club membership are modest—one nice party, for example—they will cost money. Even if premiums are donated, you still will be stuck with the handling and shipping. The point is that every expense related to the contribution reduces its value to you.
3. Clubs and premiums can backfire if you do not deliver what you promise. If contributors do not receive the club benefits or the premiums they were led to expect, they may act like disappointed lovers. Their position will be that they kept their part of the bargain by mailing in their money, but you failed to keep yours. Expect to be reminded of this the next time you ask them for money—if you do not hear about it before. In addition, potential contributors will interpret these lapses as a sign of poor organization, and nobody wants to support a poorly organized group.
4. For clubs and premiums to work well and to be cost effective, precious time must be devoted to them. Staff and volunteers working on this are not available for other important tasks. For example, the person who is busy arranging for the mailing out of premiums may not have time to help organize pledge collection. Obviously, the latter is far more important to the success of your program.
5. Some contributors think that money spent on clubs and premiums is money spent foolishly. These people usually are your true believers, who would prefer seeing the money you collect go straight to the cause without being sidetracked. That you offer membership in clubs and send out premiums may actually encourage these people not to contribute as much.

Now that you know about both the advantages and disadvantages of using clubs and premiums, we wish we could provide you with a firm rule about using them. Unfortunately, we cannot. Whether or not you should use clubs and premiums depends entirely on your situation. You will be able to determine this, however, by asking yourself one simple question: do we need clubs and/or premiums to provide potential contributors with an additional incentive to give or do they already have sufficient incentive?

- If your program does not offer the installment option because you need the money immediately, you may consider using clubs and/or premiums to provide potential contributors with an additional incentive to give.

- If you are in the middle of a hotly contested political campaign, clubs and premiums rarely are necessary. Those who want to support you need no added incentive.
- If your program is falling short of its goals, clubs and/or premiums might give your program the boost it needs.
- Conversely, if your program is succeeding beyond your wildest dreams, why spend money on clubs and premiums?

These examples show you what kinds of things to consider in deciding whether you need to provide potential contributors with an additional incentive to give.

Clubs

If you decide to give clubs a try, four or five will be adequate. You will need one for major donors, two or three for middle-range contributors, and one for modest contributors.

The name of each club should reflect the level of giving of its members. You might choose descriptive names: Founders, Sustainers, and Supporters, for example. Or, you might choose names that have a special meaning for your organization. For example, at the University of Pennsylvania, those who give $1,000 or more become members of the Benjamin Franklin Society, a club named after the founder of the university.

So that clubs will not be a hollow honor, each club should have its own special benefits. The more prestigious the club, the more bountiful the benefits, of course.

The following is a list of the benefits that might accrue to club membership.

1. Special recognition. If you send your contributors a year-end report, include in that report a list of your clubs and their members. To make this really effective, you should indicate what each club signifies in terms of giving. People like to have their generosity recognized publicly. In addition, consider taking out a sizeable advertisement in a local newspaper, one read by many of your contributors, in which you publicly thank your supporters. This not only will please current supporters, but also will encourage new ones. When people see that their friends are giving you money, they are more likely to do so. If you cannot afford to publish a list of all your supporters, consider publishing a list of your major donors at least.

2. A party invitation. Invite major donors to a party. People love to mingle with their peers. You will be better off, of course, if the food and drink are donated. But if you cannot manage this, throw a party anyway. The cost is slight compared to the goodwill of major donors.

3. A publication. Send all your contributors a newsletter or similar publication regularly. This keeps them informed about your goals and how efficiently you are proceeding toward them.

4. Special privileges. For example, if you are a theater, offer your major donors a 30% discount on tickets, your middle-range contributors a 20% discount, and your modest contributors a 10% discount.

5. Premiums. Offer premiums to club members. Of course, the higher the level of giving, the more impressive the premium.

6. Membership Cards. Send all of your club members a membership card that will remind them constantly of their partnership with you. Plastic or laminated membership cards can be purchased cheaply if bought in bulk.

Select some or all of the benefits listed and match them appropriately to your clubs.

Premiums

If you decide to give premiums a try, the first step is to select those that are appropriate for your particular organization. A museum of natural history, for example, sends its contributors small replicas of dinosaurs. A women's organization sends "HELP" signs to put in the car window to alert police if the car stalls at night. Public broadcasting stations habitually send their diverse contributors a range of things from books of discount coupons to portable radios.

The best premiums are those that become mobile advertisements for your organization. When people see that others are supporting you, they are more apt to do so. Most contributors feel more comfortable sending their money to an already popular cause. When a contributor invites her neighbors in for morning coffee and serves it proudly in mugs that say, for example, Grassroots Alliance for Solar Energy, she may be the first in her circle to have mugs like that—but she probably will not be the last.

You will need to select a range of premiums, each one reflecting a different level of giving, similar to the way that clubs reflect different levels of giving. A $500 contributor will not be satisfied with a bumper sticker, for example. Save that for the $25 contributor. Offer no more than five different premiums, however. Otherwise the enterprise will become too complex.

It is essential to come up with new premiums periodically and discontinue others. Steady contributors become bored if your premiums are the same year after year. (How many tote bags does one need?) Also, if you habitually discontinue premiums after a suitable length of time, contributors will come to know that if they are longing for a certain premium, they had better come up with a pledge now and not put you off.

As a rule of thumb, do not spend more for a premium than 5% of the contribution. If this seems tightfisted, keep in mind that on top of that 5% you will have handling and shipping expenses. Remember, every expense related to the contribution reduces its value to you.

Better yet, try to get the premiums donated. You can negotiate for premiums much as you do for money. Emphasize how good the contributor will feel doing his share for the cause and how valuable his gift of premiums will be because it will help bring in larger contributions than you would get without it. Name drop: tell him who else is donating premiums, especially if those names have meaning for him.

If he does not want to give you as many premiums as you need, negotiate around quantity, going down slowly just as you would if you were talking about dollars. The following is a model on which to base your negotiations for premiums. Study it and invent ones of your own for practice until you get the hang of it.

CALLER: John, I hope the Rockets can give us a block of tickets to give away as premiums like they did last year. They were hot items, those tickets. People were practically standing in line to give us money for the disabled vets when they found out what the premium was.

POTENTIAL CONTRIBUTOR: Well now, I haven't been thinking about it. Too much else on my mind.

CALLER: The thing that is so good about it for you is that the Rockets can't buy the kind of publicity they get when we put their name on every one of the flyers that we send out announcing the fund raiser. That means they're listed right alongside of the other big enterprises that make Sacramento the great city it is.

POTENTIAL CONTRIBUTOR: I'll see what I can come up with.

CALLER: Can I have your promise today, John? That way I can let the people at the Legion know about it right away.

POTENTIAL CONTRIBUTOR: Let's see, we gave you 100 tickets last year, didn't we?

CALLER: Right, and I was hoping this year you could double that since the tickets made such a hit with our contributors and since you got so much great publicity out of it.

POTENTIAL CONTRIBUTOR: Don't you ever give a guy a break? Half the
  people in the city are after us for freebees. You're not the only ones.
CALLER: I know what you're up against, John. But I also know you like to
  do the best you can to make Sacramento a place where people care
  about one another. Am I right?
POTENTIAL CONTRIBUTOR: Okay, you got your tickets. But 150 will be the
  best I can do.
CALLER: Terrific! Thanks!

One last note: If you decide to give clubs and/or premiums a try,
keep an eye on them. If you discover that they are not helping your
callers to get big pledges but instead are hurting your program, discontinue them. You will be able to make this determination by monitoring
calls. By listening to how your callers use clubs and premiums and how
potential contributors respond to them, you will know whether their
advantages outweigh their disadvantages.

How to Keep Big Gifts Coming In

Of course, all your contributors deserve heartfelt thanks. But some
clearly deserve extraspecial treatment. These are your biggest contributors, your major donors.

Who are these major donors? This is a flexible concept. Some organizations define major donors as those who give over a set dollar
amount: four times the average pledge, for example. Some organizations define major donors as those who are in the top 10% of their
contributors. The bottom line is that your major donors are your most
generous supporters. Woven throughout the book are a number of recommendations, ways to insure that major donors are given extraspecial
treatment. So that you do not have to search for them, here they are:

1. Only your best callers are allowed to call major donors. We told
   you before that this rule is necessary so that you do not throw
   away money. If an inexperienced caller calls a major donor,
   chances are that the results will not be impressive. Actually,
   there is a second reason for this rule. Not only does it insure a
   handsome pledge this year, but it insures that the major donor
   remains supportive in future years. Most of your major donors
   also will be major donors to other organizations and are used to
   being treated professionally. Inexperienced callers rarely will
   know how to handle them and therefore may cost you the
   friendship.

2. If you use clubs and premiums as negotiating tools, major donors will be eligible for the most prestigious clubs and will receive the most desirable premiums.
3. When a caller gets a big pledge—including those from major donors, of course—the director or supervisor follows up within minutes with a thank-you phone call (see page 93).
4. Everyone who honors his commitment receives an acknowledgment in addition to the thanks that is expressed in the pledge validation. For most, the acknowledgment will be a thank-you postcard. Major donors, however, are sent a special letter, not a postcard. Their substantial support justifies the additional cost. The letter is signed by someone prominent, the executive director of your organization, for example (see page 141).

Some additional ways to insure that major donors feel special are:

1. Display the names of major donors in prominent places around your organization, as hospitals do when they honor major donors by displaying their names on handsome plaques.
2. Send a list of major donors to all Board members. Encourage them to personally thank everyone they know on the list.
3. Even if your program does not use clubs, major donors should receive some of the benefits that would accrue to membership in the top-level club. For example, they should be sent invitations to special events. In addition, plan a special event—a picnic, a cocktail party, a party before or after a performance, or the like—that is strictly for major donors.

You and your staff undoubtedly will be able to come up with still more ways to please major donors. Do not overdo it, however. As precious as major donors are, the same rule applies to them that applies to other contributors: every expense related to the contribution reduces its value to you.

Clerical Workers

Just as it is important to develop a coterie of good callers, it is important to develop a conscientious clerical staff to back up the callers. Otherwise, your callers' hard work will be wasted.

Do not be shortsighted and dispense with the requisite clerical tasks if your program is a one-shot deal. Sometime in the future, probably sooner than you think, you will want to do telephone fund raising again. What will you do then if, for example, you neglected to systematically file the potential contributor records or to send thank-yous to those who pledged and paid?

The size of your clerical staff depends on the size of your program, of course. But, the same clerical tasks will present themselves, regardless of your program's size, although their quantity will differ. These tasks are already familiar to you. They include:

1. Sending the pledge validations which, of course, must be mailed the day after pledges are made, no later.
2. Sending notices that installment payments are due.
3. Filing the potential contributor records of those who pledge. (Remember you will need two separate filing systems: one for notifying potential contributors when installment payments come due and the other for collecting overdue pledges.)
4. Marking the potential contributor records with "pd" and the date of receipt as money comes in.
5. Refiling the records of potential contributors who have paid the full amount pledged.
6. Sending reminders to those who pledged three weeks before but have not paid.
7. Pulling the records of potential contributors who pledged six weeks before but have not paid so that they may be called.
8. Sending thank-yous promptly.
9. Pulling from the installment notice and pledge collection files the records of those potential contributors who deny ever having made a pledge.
10. Pulling the file of potential contributor records that is dated eight weeks prior to the current date and removing the corresponding potential contributor records from the alphabetical files. (These are the potential contributors who have not paid even after the pledge collection process has been completed.)
11. Sorting the records of potential contributors (by list, for example) who could not be reached during a calling session so that they can be called again during the very next session.
12. Doing phone research.
13. Assisting the director with record keeping. (The following section examines record keeping.)

As you know, the first 11 tasks must be done every day.

Rely on volunteers rather than on paid workers to do these clerical tasks. If your program is sizeable, however, you should consider paying at least one key clerical worker who will be there regularly to insure that the volunteers are working productively. To attract a capable person, pay at least 50¢ an hour more than the minimum wage and allow for salary mobility.

To organize the work so that it will attract enthusiastic volunteers, begin by listing everything you want them to do for you—augmenting, if need be, the basic list you just read. Next, write job descriptions for each task. When a volunteer realizes you have gone to the trouble of writing a detailed job description, he will know he is not giving up his time for "make work." In addition, writing job descriptions will force you to think about how long various tasks take to perform. It is unfair to assign a task to a volunteer, nonchalantly minimizing how long it will take, and then complain when it is done haphazardly. Most of your volunteers will feel more comfortable if they are assigned specific tasks to complete in a short period of time.

Writing down what is required for each task, both in work and in time, will seem terribly tedious when you are anxious to get your telephone fund-raising program rolling. Persevere, anyway. You need do it only once, and it will benefit you in three ways: (1) while you are doing it, you will be organizing the program subconsciously; (2) it will help you decide how many volunteers you will need and what their basic functions should be; and (3) it will be valuable while you are guiding volunteers into their proper niches. These questions will be fundamental:

1. How many volunteers should be there regularly, doing the daily tasks: filing the potential contributor records of those who pledge, for example?
2. How many volunteers should be there whenever you need them to work on substantial projects: planning a public relations campaign, for example?
3. How many volunteers should come in only now and then when you are in a predicament: to help mail out premiums if you fall behind, for example?

As valuable as volunteers are, they sometimes get on the nerves of the staff, especially if a staff member is feeling overworked and underappreciated. Volunteers may seem to be always underfoot, always asking questions. Even the volunteers themselves sometimes get annoyed and blow up. For example, at a book sale sponsored by some alumnae from a women's college, the husband of one commented on the poor weather. "What do you expect me to do about it?" barked the exhausted woman who had organized the sale. Another time, at the semiannual fund raiser of a children's hospital, a hard-working volunteer was taking a short breather when he was commanded by a high-strung staff member to grab a broom and sweep the floor.

Outrageous episodes like these can never be stopped entirely, but everyone involved in your program, volunteers and staff alike, should be taught that unhappy volunteers never stay around. They should all understand that every day is "Appreciate the Volunteers Day."

Although clerical work should be task-oriented, do not set up your program like an assembly line with each person responsible for only one facet of it, oblivious to the rest. Each person may have one area of responsibility—sending reminders, for example—but he should know what the other people do and how his responsibilities affect theirs.

The assembly line method seems efficient in the short run when you are straining to get your program under way quickly. It works out poorly in the long run, however, because if even one part flounders, the whole program is apt to suffer. Again, sending reminders is a perfect example. If the reminders are not sent on time, expect your cash flow to become sluggish and some pledges to be lost completely. As a result, you may not be able to be generous with bonus money. Therefore, the callers may not negotiate aggressively. This will bring on a further decline in the program's productivity.

Especially when your program depends on volunteers, it is important that others have the know-how to step into the breach if a volunteer does not show up. Volunteers usually take to diversification of duties with enthusiasm. Because they are not getting the stimulation of a paycheck, they like the stimulation of switching tasks often.

The bulk of the clerical tasks cannot be postponed. They need to be done like clockwork, day after day. If you begin to get behind and volunteers are scarce, quickly hire some part-time workers until you catch up or locate more volunteers. One of the advantages of part-time help is that it can be added or subtracted with relative ease to accommodate the work flow. The calling coterie itself is the first place to look when you need to add clerical workers. Some of the callers probably will be available, and by doing clerical tasks during the day they will learn more about how telephone fund raising works and will become better callers.

When you look for clerical help, whether it is unpaid or paid, look for dependability ahead of special skills. If applicants are faithful, willing workers, take them gratefully. You can teach them what they need to know. It is not difficult, for instance, to train people to stuff envelopes.

A few words about phone number research: if you cannot get the lists you want with phone numbers, you will be obliged to do considerable phone number research, defined as calling directory assistance or using the phone book to find potential contributors' correct phone numbers. Researchers calling directory assistance should be able to come up with approximately 50 numbers per hour. Even if you can buy the lists you want complete with phone numbers, you will need to do regular phone number research. Every night potential contributor records will surface bearing the names of people whose phone number no longer is current. Researchers should do their best to find current numbers for these people as soon as possible so the value of the lead postcard is not negated.

Phone number research is less cut and dried than you might suspect. After your researchers have a month or so of experience, call a meeting so they can compare notes about how to interact productively with directory assistance employees, who, like everyone else, are sometimes resentful, impatient, or just plain tired. This meeting will probably be so helpful that you will want to call another in several months, or sooner, if you hire new researchers. In addition, the researchers will be pleased that you value their ideas. Doing phone number research is unexciting work. Meeting with them will help them see the worth of what they are doing.

As an alternative to in-house phone number research, you may wish to consider having it done by an outside company specializing in phone number research. One way to find these companies is in fund raising magazines (see page 110) where they advertise frequently.

A few words on filing as well. Maintaining accurate and up-to-date files can be time consuming and tedious. Nonetheless, it is imperative that your files be accurate and up-to-date, for if they are not, your program will lose money. Accurate and up-to-date files insure that installment payments come in on time, that delinquent pledges are collected, and that current contributors are not called too soon after their previous gift.

Two more points, the first on organization: organize the paper room so that it is easy to find the potential contributor records one needs. The shelves must be labeled and the labels must be easy to read.

The second point: with all the mailing of validations, installment-due notices, and reminders, you will need quantities of envelopes. You can use the less-costly window envelopes as return envelopes if the validation and the reminder are designed to be compatible with them. In other words, when potential contributors return their checks, they can

simply insert them into the envelope along with the validation or reminder, and your address will show through the window in the way
familiar to us all. To economize still further, you should have the envelopes, validations, installment-due notices, reminders, potential contributor records, and postcards printed in the largest quantity feasible. Obli-
ging printers and letter shops sometimes will store supplies for good
customers.

Record Keeping

Every program needs records and yours is no exception. But keeping records should not be an end in itself. Only keep records that will
help you plan and administer your program. The following pages contain suggestions for records concerning the callers, the program, and the
potential contributors. Maintain these records even if your program is a
one-shot deal. Do not be shortsighted. While they may not help you in
your current effort, if you decide to have another one-shot deal or to use
telephone fund raising in an ongoing way, they will be indispensable.
For example, not only will they tell you who your most productive
callers were, but they also will tell you who your most generous potential contributors were. Without these two essential pieces of information, you would need to begin your next telephone fund-raising program from scratch.

Of course, you need not compile these records during your one-
shot deal, when every minute is taken up. Compile them shortly after it
is over, when you have time to catch your breath.

Caller Records

Keep track of these statistics for each caller: average pledge, pledge
rate, and dollars raised per session. These numbers, in conjunction with
the caller evaluations (which are the product of the monitoring process),
will help you decide to whom to give a raise and whom to dismiss.

To make these calculations, you will need to know the number of
dollars raised, the number of calls completed, and the number of
pledges secured by the caller over a given period. (A completed call is
one in which the caller makes direct contact with the potential contributor and no further telephone contact between the two is necessary.
There are two kinds of completed calls: pledges and nonpledges.)

Each caller should fill out a Totals Sheet at the end of every calling
session to provide you with this information, such as on page 165.

Totals

Calling station phone no.: _____

Caller's name: _____

Date: _____

Number of calls completed: _____

Number of pledges: _____

Dollars pledged: _____

Pledges by amount: _____ _____ _____ _____ _____

_____ _____ _____ _____ _____ _____ _____

_____ _____ _____ _____ _____ _____ _____

_____ _____ _____ _____ _____ _____ _____

If the calls are made during the day, the caller should write "Day Calls" at the top of the sheet.

To calculate the caller's average pledge for a given period, divide the total number of dollars raised by the number of pledges made during the same period. To calculate her pledge rate for a given period, divide the number of pledges made by the number of calls completed during the same period. To calculate the dollars raised per session for a given period, divide the total number of dollars pledged by the number of sessions held in the same period.

For example, let's say Susan calls Monday and Tuesday from 6:30 to 9:30 and her Totals Sheets are as appears on pages 167 and 168. Susan's weekly totals would be:

- Number of calls completed   43 (23 + 20)
- Number of pledges   14 (6 + 8)
- Dollars pledged $980 ($510 + $470)
- Average pledge $70 ($980 ÷ 14)
- Pledge rate   32% (14 ÷ 43)
- Dollars raised per session $490 ($980 ÷ 2)
- Number of sessions   2 (1 + 1)

Use the chart on page 169 as a model to house this information:

As you can see, the chart includes weekly, monthly, and cumulative statistics. Weekly statistics tell you how your callers are currently doing. Monthly statistics, on the other hand, tell you how your callers have done over time so you can see whether their performance is improving, declining, or remaining steady.

To calculate a caller's monthly and cumulative totals, add the number of calls completed, number of pledges, dollars pledged, and number of sessions for the current week to the caller's previous monthly and cumulative totals. Then calculate her average pledge, pledge rate, and dollars raised per session just as you calculate the weekly totals.

So if Susan's Caller Record for the previous week looked like the chart on page 170, then her new record, taking into account her two additional nights of calling, would be the one shown on page 171.

What do these numbers tell you? First, that Susan is an overall good caller, and second, that her performance is consistently improving.

Compare Susan's record with Tony's on page 172.

As you can see, Tony is a new caller who is off to a weak start. His cumulative average pledge is fine ($55.88), but his cumulative pledge rate is low (15%). Equally important, the number of calls he completes per three-hour session, 29, is too high. (Number of calls completed

Totals

Calling station phone no. __7272__

Caller's name: __SUSAN BROWN__

Date: __9-18-86__

Number of calls completed: __23__

Number of pledges: __8__

Dollars pledged: __$470__

Pledges by amount: __60__ __100__ __50__ __70__ __25__

__40__ __35__ __90__ ____ ____ ____ ____

Totals

Calling station phone no.: __7276__

Caller's name: __SUSAN BROWN__

Date: __9-19-86__

Number of calls completed: __20__

Number of pledges: __6__

Dollars pledged: __$ 510__

Pledges by amount: __200__ __150__ __50__ __50__ __35__

__25__ ____ ____ ____ ____ ____

____ ____ ____ ____ ____ ____

____ ____ ____ ____ ____ ____

Caller Record

Caller:	Week:	Month:	Cumulative from:
Number of calls completed			
Number of pledges			
Dollars pledged			
Average pledge			
Pledge rate			
Dollars raised per session			
Number of sessions			

Caller Record

Caller: SUSAN BROWN	Week: 9-11-86	Month: SEPTEMBER	Cumulative from: 7-3-86
Number of calls completed	61	104	360
Number of pledges	20	37	123
Dollars pledged	$1090	$2245	$7165
Average pledge	$54.50	$60.68	$58.25
Pledge rate	33%	36%	34%
Dollars raised per session	363	449	421
Number of sessions	3	5	17

Caller Record

Caller: SUSAN BROWN	Week: 9-18-86	Month: SEPTEMBER	Cumulative from: 7-3-86
Number of calls completed	43	147	403
Number of pledges	14	51	137
Dollars pledged	$980	$3225	$8145
Average pledge	$70	$63.24	$59.45
Pledge rate:	32%	35%	34%
Dollars raised per session	$490	$461	$429
Number of sessions	2	7	19

Caller Record

Caller: TONY WILLISTON	Week: 9-18-86	Month: SEPTEMBER	Cumulative from: 9-2-86
Number of calls completed	58	114	114
Number of pledges	9	17	17
Dollars pledged	$490	950	950
Average pledge	$54.44	$55.88	$55.88
Pledge rate	16%	15%	15%
Dollars raised per session	245	238	238
Number of sessions	2	4	4

divided by number of sessions equals numbers of calls completed per session.) Remember, callers should complete about seven completed calls per hour, not nine or ten. The low pledge rate coupled with the high contact rate suggests that Tony is rushing through negotiations. His caller evaluations probably will confirm this.

Not only is it important to know how each caller is doing individually, but you need to know how his performance compares with that of the rest of the group. Callers with similar records and evaluations should be treated similarly with regard to giving them raises and dismissing them. Rank callers by the amount of money they raise per session, their average pledge, and their pledge rate using the chart on page 174.

Completed, the chart would resemble the one on page 175.

The statistics used to put together for the Caller Rankings come from the Caller Records. You also may wish to rank your callers based on their monthly and/or cumulative totals.

As we pointed out, callers with similar records and evaluations should be treated similarly with regard to giving them raises and dismissing them. An example based on the above rankings illustrates this point. If you raise Green from $5.50 to $6.00, do the same for Weiss. Likewise, if you let Burger go, let Landau go as well, unless Landau is a new caller who, unlike Burger, has not yet had a fair opportunity to prove his worth. Of course, you would not change a caller's status based on weekly statistics unless those statistics reflect his performance over time.

Do not post your caller rankings in full. There is no need to embarrass weak callers. If a caller is doing poorly, let her go, but do not humiliate her. While you do not want to display the entire caller rankings, you do want to recognize excellence. Accordingly, post the top one third of the chart conspicuously.

Also, keep track of bonus money. After each calling session, fill out a chart like that on page 176.

Completed, the chart would resemble the one on page 177.

You will notice that a few of the bonuses were marked "pd." As you know, unlike bonuses for high nightly totals, which are paid immediately, bonuses for individual pledges are not paid until the pledge (or the first installment) is paid. When the check arrives and the bonus is paid, indicate it on the chart. Save the charts in case of a dispute.

One more calculation: dollars raised per caller per session. As you will recall, you need to know this number when you give your callers notice that their job performance is unsatisfactory (see pages 100 and

Caller Rankings

Week:			
	Dollars raised per session	Average pledge	Pledge rate
1			
2			
3			
4			
5			
6			
7			
8			
9			
10			
11			
12			

Caller Rankings

	Dollars raised per session	Average pledge	Pledge rate
1	GREEN $620	GREEN $73.22	WEISS 49%
2	WEISS $590	BROWN $70.	GREEN 45%
3	WARD $545	WEISS $68.43	WARD 43%
4	LASKY $520	LASKY $68.31	DAVIS 41%
5	BROWN $490	BACON $57.08	BROWN 32%
6	DAVIS $460	WARD $55.12	LASKY 30%
7	BACON $390	WILLISTON $54.44	BACON 23%
8	BEAVER $353	DAVIS $52.54	BEAVER 20%
9	WILLISTON $245	BEAVER $46.10	RICO 19%
10	RICO $190	RICO $40.59	BURGER 17%
11	BURGER $130	BURGER $38.15	WILLISTON 16%
12	LANDAU $110	LANDAU $36	LANDAU 13%

Week: 9-11-86

Bonus Dollars for:		
Nightly totals	Dollar amount	Bonus
#1		
#2		
#3		
Large pledges		
1		
2		
3		
4		
5		
6		
7		

Bonus Dollars for: **9-11-86**		
Nightly totals	Dollar amount	Bonus
#1 GREEN	$ 720	$ 6
#2 WEISS	$ 690	$ 4
#3 BROWN	$ 630	$ 3
Large pledges		
1 GREEN	$ 400	$ 4 pd.
2 GREEN	$ 300	$ 3
3 BROWN	$ 300	$ 3 pd.
4 WEISS	$ 200	$ 2 pd.
5 WARD	$ 200	$ 2
6		
7		

102) or if you decide to offer bonus money to any caller who raises in a given session at least 1.5 times the threshold amount [the threshold amount is the dollars raised per caller per session (see page 95)].

Follow these two steps to calculate this figure:

1. Calculate the dollars raised per session for each of your callers (except for those callers who were let go for unsatisfactory performance) for the previous month.
2. Add up those numbers and divide by the number of callers. This will give you the dollars raised per session per caller.

So let's say in January you had eight callers, but let one go, and the dollars raised per session for the remaining seven callers were as follows: $170, $220, $360, $240, $500, $620, and $345. Your dollars per session per caller would be $351 ($2455 ÷ 7).

Calculate this number at the end of each month and use the calculation for the subsequent month.

Program Records

In addition to maintaining records on individual callers, keep records on the program. Use these records to gauge the progress of your program and to chart its direction. Do the following:

1. Keep track of total dollars pledged, the average pledge, and pledge rate and dollars raised per session. Use the chart on page 179 as a model.

As you can see, the chart provides the same basic statistics as the Caller Record does. But instead of telling you how an individual caller is doing, it tells you how your program is doing.

Use the callers' totals sheets to determine the number of calls completed, the number of pledges made, and the dollars pledged for the week. Then calculate the average pledge, the pledge rate, and the dollars pledged per session. To refresh your memory, calculate the average pledge for a given period by dividing the dollars raised by the number of pledges made during the same period. To calculate the pledge rate for a given period, divide the number of pledges made by the number of calls completed during the same period. To calculate the dollars pledged per session for a given period, divide dollars pledged by the number of sessions during that same period.

2. If you are calling a variety of groups of potential contributors, you will want to keep track of each group's effectiveness. Do so by filling out a separate progress report for each group. Label these clearly so you

Program Progress Report

Caller:	Week:	Month:	Year:	Cumulative from:
Number of calls completed				
Number of pledges				
Dollars pledged				
Average pledge				
Pledge rate				
Dollars raised per session				
Number of sessions				

do not confuse one progress report with another. Note the examples on pages 181–184.

The chart clearly shows that potential contributors from Source A are the most generous, while those from Source C are the least generous. Compare their monthly totals:

Pledge rate:
Source A—43%
Source C—21%

Average pledge:
Source A—$76.25
Source C—$32.40

Share this information with your list broker the next time you need names.

The chart also clearly shows that the potential contributors from Source B are becoming increasingly less generous. Look at their declining pledge rate:

Week—31%
Month—35%
Year—39%
Cumulative—39%

Monitor the calls to this group closely to try to figure out why it is becoming increasingly less generous.

You may wish to rank your groups of potential contributors in the same way that you rank your callers: average pledge and pledge rate as on page 185.

3. You need to know not only how much money is pledged, but also how much money actually comes in. The second statistic is obviously more important than the first. You cannot pay your bills with pledges. Use the chart on page 186 as a model to help keep track of how much money has come in.

There will be a disparity between what has been pledged and what has come in on any given date because people do not pay their pledges the day they make them. Still, to determine how solid your pledges are, you need to know the pledge fulfillment rate. If your program does not use installments, you can figure out the pledge fulfillment rate by comparing the dollars pledged on any given date with the amount of money that has actually come in two months from that date. Allow two months so that the results of pledge collection will be reflected fully. If a delinquent potential contributor has not sent in his money by two weeks after the

Potential Contributor Group Progress Report

SOURCE A	Week: 8-15	Month: AUGUST	Year: 1986	Cumulative from: MAY 86
Number of calls completed	80	170	895	895
Number of pledges	36	73	394	394
Dollars pledged	$2550	$5566	$29,700	$29,700
Average pledge	$70.83	$76.25	$75.38	$75.38
Pledge rate	45%	43%	44%	44%

Potential Contributor Group Progress Report

SOURCE B	Week: 8-15	Month: AUGUST	Year: 1986	Cumulative from: MAY 86
Number of calls completed	90	200	865	865
Number of pledges	28	70	337	337
Dollars pledged	$1200	$3017	$14,570	$14,570
Average pledge	$42.86	$43.10	$43.23	$43.23
Pledge rate	31 %	35%	39%	39%

Potential Contributor Group Progress Report

SOURCE C	Week: 8-15	Month: AUGUST	Year: 1986	Cumulative from: MAY 86
Number of calls completed	65	142	660	660
Number of pledges	12	30	145	145
Dollars pledged	$420	$972	$4960	$4960
Average pledge	$35.00	$32.40	$34.21	$34.21
Pledge rate	18%	21%	22%	22%

Potential Contributor Group Progress Report

SOURCE D	Week: 8-15	Month: AUGUST	Year: 1986	Cumulative from: MAY 1986
Number of calls completed	93	180	910	910
Number of pledges	28	55	282	282
Dollars pledged	$1,428	$2,795	$14,390	$14,390
Average pledge	$51.00	$50.82	$50.13	$51.03
Pledge rate	30%	31%	31%	31%

Potential Contributor Rankings by Group

Week: **8-15-86**

	Average pledge	Pledge rate
1	Source A $70.83	Source A 45%
2	Source D $51.00	Source B 31%
3	Source B $42.86	Source D 30%
4	Source C $35.00	Source C 18%
5		
6		
7		
8		
9		
10		
11		
12		

Money Received

	Week:	Month:	Year:	Cumulative from:
Dollars received				

pledge collection call (in other words, by two months from the date of his pledge), chances are his money will never come in. If the pledge fulfillment rate is 80% or more, you are doing well. So, if $300,000 was pledged as of May 1 and $240,000 came in by July 1, you have nothing to worry about. No matter how carefully pledges are validated and no matter how thorough pledge collection is, some people will renege on their pledge.

Naturally, if your program uses installments, the pledge fulfillment rate always will be slightly lower because only a portion of the pledge is paid immediately. Keep a cautious eye on installments to make sure that the later installments come in with the same regularity as the earlier installments. Like the first installment, the subsequent installments are commitments. Your callers must convey that idea to your contributors.

There is no need to keep track of dollars collected by potential contributor group. This is because the pledge fulfillment rate generally does not vary significantly among groups of potential contributors.

4. Maintain a budget. A model to use when constructing your own is shown on page 187.

5. Pledge collection: It is not necessary to maintain formal pledge collection records. If pledge collection is working, this will be reflected in a high pledge-fulfillment rate. So that you can reassure yourself of this with a quick glance through the day's mail, consider using color-coded or otherwise coded pledge collection return envelopes.

Do not maintain elaborate records on your telephone pledge collectors either. It will suffice if each pledge collector fills out a Totals Sheet during each session. The sheet should give the following information:

- The number of calls completed. Pledge collection calls average between two to three minutes. This is in contrast to telephone

Budget

	Month		Quarter		Year	
	A	S	A	S	A	S
Caller payroll						
Clerical payroll						
Administrative payroll						
Advertising						
List broker						
Letter shop						
Office supplies						
Telephones						

A = Allocated;   S = Spent

fund-raising calls which average between three to seven minutes. Because pledge collection calls are shorter, more can be completed per hour. Expect approximately nine completed pledge collection calls per hour.

- The number of pledges that potential contributors promise to pay in as well as the number of dollars these pledges represent.
- The number of renegotiated pledges that potential contributors promise to pay and the number of dollars these pledges represent, as well as the original value of these pledges. If your callers are doing a good job, you should see a number of renegotiated pledges each session.
- The number of pledges that potential contributors claim they already have sent in, as well as the number of dollars these pledges represent. If this number is significant, it may suggest that your clerical workers are not doing their job properly. Otherwise, payment would have been noted. We use the word "may" because sometimes potential contributors will claim to have sent in their payments even though it is not true.
- The number of pledges that potential contributors refuse to pay, as well as the number of dollars these pledges represent.

A sample Pledge Collection Totals Sheet is shown on page 189. Completed, it would resemble the one on page 190.

By looking at a pledge collector's Totals Sheets and by monitoring her occasionally, you will know whether she is doing a satisfactory job. Pledge collectors do not compete for bonus money or for raises. Therefore, you do not need to keep close track of the amount of money they collect each session nor do you need to rank them. Indeed, ranking pledge collectors fairly is impossible because their results are to some extent predetermined by the actions of the initial callers.

6. Refusal analysis: You should maintain the records just described in an ongoing way. In addition, you may want to analyze particular aspects of your program intermittently. For example, you may want to find out why potential contributors refuse to pledge.

When a potential contributor does not respond to a direct mail solicitation, the reason for the refusal is a mystery. This usually is not the case with telephone fund raising. In most cases, the potential contributor who decides not to give will volunteer the reason. In those rare cases when this information is not volunteered, the telephone fund

Pledge Collection Totals

Calling station phone no.: _____

Caller's name: _____

Date: _____

Number of calls completed: _____

Will send in full amount: _____   _____
                                            Number   Amount

Will send in renegotiated pledge: _____   _____
                                            Number   Amount

                                            _____
                                            Amount pledged originally

Already sent in pledge: _____   _____
                                            Number   Amount

Will not send in pledge: _____   _____
                                            Number   Amount

Why not?:

  A. Financial problems: _____   _____
                                            Number   Amount

  B. Denies making pledge: _____   _____
                                            Number   Amount

  C. Other: _____   _____
                                            Number   Amount

Pledge Collection Totals

Calling station phone no.: _234-5677_

Caller's name: _ELLEN MARKS_

Date: _10-12-86_

Number of calls completed: _29 (during three hours of calling)_

Will send in full amount: _15_   _$820_
                                  Number   Amount

Will send in renegotiated pledge: _4_   _$210_
                                  Number   Amount

                                   _$370_
                           Amount pledged originally

Already sent in pledge: _2_   _$110_
                                  Number   Amount

Will not send in pledge: _8_   _$580_
                                  Number   Amount

Why not?:

  A. Financial problems: _5_   _$410_
                                  Number   Amount

  B. Denies making pledge: _2_   _$120_
                                  Number   Amount

  C. Other: _1_   _$50_
                                  Number   Amount

raiser can uncover it with a simple question: "May I ask why you have decided not to support us this year?"

There are certain standard reasons for refusal that hold true for all organizations. They are:

- Lack of funds. The potential contributor supports your organization philosophically, but does not have the resources to stand behind his philosophical commitment.
- Lack of interest. The potential contributor is not interested in your organization.
- Other priorities. The potential contributor believes in your cause and has the resources to support it, but believes that other organizations are either more worthy or more needy.
- Will not make a commitment. The potential contributor has a policy against making a commitment concerning money over the phone and refuses to make an exception to this policy despite your persuasive efforts. Occasionally, potential contributors may refuse to make a commitment for reasons that apply specifically to your organization. They usually will relate to a policy, program, or person in your organization.

You can discover the most common reasons for refusal by talking to some of your better callers. They will be able to convey a general overview. But sometimes you will want more than a rough accounting. You will need hard and fast numbers. For example, if a particular group of potential contributors is not living up to expectations or if your organization has instituted a controversial policy or program and you want to see if that is costing you money, you probably should conduct a refusal analysis.

Use experienced, top-notch callers. Do not use mediocre or new callers. Keeping track of refusals is much easier than negotiating pledges. If new or mediocre callers are asked to do both, they will concentrate on the former at the expense of the latter. You will end up with a wealth of information and a dearth of dollars. On the other hand, your top-notch callers (who are vying for bonus money) will not let this simple task distract them from the all-important goal of raising money.

Prepare a Refusal Tally Sheet. Talk to your better callers and come up with a list of six or seven of the most common reasons for refusal. Do not forget the generic reasons that were previously discussed, such as a policy of never making a commitment concerning money over the phone, for example. List these reasons on the tally sheet. The tally sheet also should provide callers with space to list additional reasons as they come across them during calls. If you discover that you omitted an important reason or included an unimportant one, adjust the tally sheet. A sample tally sheet is shown on page 193.

As you can see, the first four complaints are generic; the second three are specific to the institution. You also will notice a space for the potential contributor group. You might want to instruct your callers to keep track of all refusals. Or you might want to narrow your study to a particular group of potential contributors. You might want to know, for example, why potential contributors from a particular geographic area or from a particular list are refusing to give. This is why the callers will need to indicate which group of potential contributors they are calling: general, Scottsdale, List B, and so on.

Completed, the tally sheet resembles the one on page 194.

After each week, total the results. Also, calculate what percentage of the total number of refusals each category constitutes. (To arrive at this percentage, divide the number of refusals in each category by the total number of refusals in all categories.) Use the chart on page 195 as a model.

Completed, the chart would resemble the one on page 196.

What does the above analysis tell you? By looking at the cumulative numbers, the following is clear:

1. There is no need to continue the refusal analysis. Clear patterns have emerged.
2. The College's admission policy and recent selection of Everett Kingsley as provost are not significant problems. They account for only 4% and 3%, respectively, of the refusals.
3. The study also tells you that few people object to the telephone fund-raising process. Only 5% would not make a commitment over the phone. No more than 5% ever should refuse for this reason. Your callers should be able to convince potential contributors that you are worthy of their making an exception to their general policy of not committing over the phone.
4. Clearly, the College's investment policy is its greatest fund-raising obstacle. If you discover that a particular policy, program, or person in your organization is costing you money, do two things. First, notify the policy planners (in this case, the trustees). Because you depend on the public for at least a percentage of your support, what the public thinks is important. Policy planners and decision makers can use the information you collect to perform their functions better. Second, use this information when you work with your callers. Emphasize the problem at

Benjamin Stoddart College Refusal Tally Sheet

Calling station phone no.: _____

Caller's name: _____

Date: _____

Potential contributor group: _____

Number of refusals: _____

Reasons for refusal:

1. No interest: _____   _____

2. No money: _____   _____

3. Other priorities: _____   _____

4. Will not commit over the phone: _____   _____

5. Objects to the college's investment

   policy: _____   _____

6. Objects to the college's admission

   policy: _____   _____

7. Objects to the college's selection of Everett

   Kingsley as new provost: _____   _____

8. Other: _____   _____

   _____   _____

   _____   _____

   _____   _____

   _____   _____

Benjamin Stoddart College Refusal Tally Sheet

Calling station phone no.: _234-5678_

Caller's name: __J. STARR__

Date: _9-12-86_

Potential contributor group: _GENERAL_

Number of refusals: _8_

Reasons for refusal:

1. No interest: _✔✔✔_   _3_

2. No money: _✔_   _1_

3. Other priorities: _____   _0_

4. Will not commit over the phone: _✔_   _1_

5. Objects to the college's investment

   policy: _✔✔_   _2_

6. Objects to the college's admission

   policy: _____   _0_

7. Objects to the college's selection of Everett

   Kingsley as new provost: _✔_   _1_

8. Other: _____   _____

   _____   _____

   _____   _____

   _____   _____

   _____   __(8)__

Refusal Analysis

	Week:		Cumulative from:	
	No.	%	No.	%
Totals: 1. No interest				
2. No money				
3. Other priorities				
4. Will not make a commitment over phone				
5. Objects to investment policy				
6. Objects to admission policy				
7. Objects to the selection of Everett Kingsley as provost				
8. Other				
Total number of refusals _____				

Refusal Analysis

	Week:		Cumulative from:	
	No.	%	No.	%
Totals:	76	100%	166	100%
1. No interest	9	12%	21	13%
2. No money	26	35%	57	34%
3. Other priorities	3	4%	8	5%
4. Will not make a commitment over phone	4	5%	8	5%
5. Objects to investment policy	21	35%	60	36%
6. Objects to admission policy	4	5%	7	4%
7. Objects to the selection of Everett Kingsley as provost	3	4%	5	3%
8. Other	0	0%	0	0%
Total number of refusals _____				

training. Incorporate it into the Common Problems handout. And discuss it with the callers as a group.

5. The potential contributors' lack of money is the next greatest fund-raising obstacle. This accounted for 35% of the refusals. This always will account for between one third to one half of your refusals. Note well, however, that this figure applies only to refusals, not to calls completed.

6. No matter how worthy your cause and how dynamic your organization, there will be some potential contributors who lack interest. This group usually will account for between 10% and 25% of your refusals. In the College's refusal study, they account for 13%, an acceptable figure. Note again that this figure applies specifically to refusals, not to calls completed.

7. Five percent of the potential contributors had higher giving priorities. If this number is 10% or over, you have a problem. If your callers are negotiating firmly, few potential contributors should get away with this.

The Potential Contributor Record

As you already know, each potential contributor has a potential contributor record. The record tracks the movement of the potential contributor through the telephone fund-raising system. Use the chart on pages 198 through 200 as a model.

As you can see, page 1 of the potential contributor record deals with the process of getting a pledge; page 2, with the actual pledge; and page three, with pledge collection. A section by section analysis follows. Of course, that which is obvious is not analyzed.

Page 1:
1. *Potential contributor identification*
   - *Source code:* This is where you indicate the potential contributor group. For example, potential contributors from Cherry Hill might be designated as "CH" while potential contributors from Lansdale might be designated "LD."
   - *Sequence number:* This is the potential contributor's computer number.
   - *Calling date:* A potential contributor can be called five days after the postcard is mailed. Indicate that date on the potential contributor record so that the potential contributor is not called before the postcard arrives.

Potential Contributor Record

Identification:			Changes:		
Name:					
Address:					
Phone:					
Source code:					
Sequence no:					
Calling date:			☐ Day call		

Caller activity:

	Name	Date	Time	NA	NDC	Complete
1						
2						
3						
4						
5						
6						
7						
8						

Outcome:

Pledge ☐

Refusal ☐

Unreachable ☐

Notes:

Pledge Information

Date: _____

Caller: _____

Amount: _____

Time: _____

Matching gift co.: _____

Credit card number
  and co.: _____

Credit card expiration
  date: _____

Payment plan:

  All at once

  Semiannually

  Quarterly

Pledge collection

Reminder:

Telephone follow-up:

	Name	Date	Time	NA	NDC	Complete
1						
2						
3						
4						
5						
6						
7						
8						

Outcome:

Will send in ☐ (amount)

Already sent in ☐ (amount)

Unreachable ☐

Will not send in ☐

  Why not?:

  Financial problem ☐

  Denies making pledge ☐

  Other _____

Payment:

2. *Changes:* If there is a change of name, address, or phone number, this should be indicated legibly in the space provided. If this change turns the call into a day call, check the day call box.

3. *Caller activity:*

- No potential contributor should be called more than eight times. If a potential contributor has not been reached by the eighth call, designate him as unreachable.
- NA stands for no answer. NDC stands for no direct contact (if, for example, you speak with the potential contributor's husband or daughter, but not with the potential contributor).
- If a caller completes a call, he should indicate it and in addition fill in the outcome section of the potential contributor record.

4. *Outcome*

- Unreachable, as you know, indicates that the potential contributor has not been reached after eight calls.
- Refusals are potential contributors who do not pledge.
- If the potential contributor pledges, the caller should fill in the Pledge Information section.

5. *Notes:* Any relevant information about the potential contributor should be noted here; for example, his interests, his working hours, and so on.

6. *Prior giving history:* This was not indicated on the potential contributor record. Callers have a tendency, a bad tendency, to assume that a potential contributor can give no more than his prior gift. As you know, this is not true. A potential contributor who gave $50 last year may very well give $200 or more this year as a result of skillful negotiating. If you give your callers information about a potential contributor's prior giving history, you run a risk they may use the information inappropriately.

If you feel compelled to let the callers know the potential contributors' prior giving histories, instruct them to remember that the amount of the prior gift is a floor, not a ceiling. Then, monitor them closely to make sure they are following instructions. In addition, compare the prior gifts with this year's gifts. If the amounts are the same or nearly the same, chances are that letting the callers know the potential contributors' prior giving histories is working against you.

Page 3:

1. *Payment:* If payment is received, write "pd" plus the date of receipt on the bottom of the page.

2. *Pledge collection:*

- If payment is not received within three weeks after the date of the pledge, send the potential contributor a reminder and indicate this by noting the date on which reminder sent.

- If the potential contributor responds to the reminder within three weeks, indicate payment at the bottom of the page.
- If the potential contributor does not respond to the reminder within three weeks, begin the telephone pledge collection process. Try calling the potential contributor at the same time of day when he made his pledge. There is a good chance he will be in. If, after eight tries, you have not yet reached the delinquent potential contributor, discontinue the collection process.
- If and when payment arrives as a result of the telephone pledge collection process, indicate payment on the bottom of the page

A complete potential contributor record appears on pages 203 through 205.

Record keeping is not as overwhelming as it may appear now. With time, maintaining records will become second nature. Your supervisor (and even your clerical workers in a pinch) can help. This will make record keeping less burdensome. The difficulty most organizations have with records is not completing them, but using them. Records have no value unless they help you plan and administer. This book gives you clear guidelines about how to use the suggested records. Follow the guidelines. Otherwise, the time you spend keeping records will go for naught.

Potential Contributor Record

Identification: Changes:

Name: JOHN EDGAR   New phone #: 572-8002

Address: 1206 Limekiln Pike
         DRESNER , North Dakota
Phone: 574 - 8711

Source code: DR

Sequence no: 8825

Calling date: 10-1-86   ☐ Day call

Caller activity:

Name	Date	Time	NA	NDC	Complete
1 STEPHENS	10/1/86	7:30	✗		
2 JACKSON	10/2/86	8:15		✗ (see note)	
3 RANDALL	10/3/86	9:20			✗
4					
5					
6					
7					
8					

Outcome:

Pledge ☒

Refusal ☐

Unreachable ☐

Notes: 10-2 Potential contributor
              works until 8:30 p.m.
              call after 9 p.m.

Pledge Information

Date: _10-3-86_

Caller: _RANDALL, G._

Amount: _$150_

Time: _9:20 p.m._

Matching gift co.: _N. A.*_

Credit card number
  and co.: _N.A._

Credit card expiration
  date: _N. A._

Payment plan:

(All at once)

Semiannually

Quarterly

*Not applicable

Pledge collection

Reminder: **Sent 10-24-86**

Telephone follow-up:

	Name	Date	Time	NA	NDC	Complete
1	VALENTINE	11-16-86	9:20	✗		
2	KEISER	11-17-86	9:30			✗
3						
4						
5						
6						
7						
8						

Outcome: ₱/150

Will send in ☒ (amount)

Already sent in ☐ (amount)

Unreachable ☐

Will not send in ☐

  Why not?:

  Financial problem ☐

  Denies making pledge ☐

  Other _____

Payment:

      ₱ 150 pd. (11-22-86)

EPILOGUE

HOW TO USE THE PHONE TO
DO ALMOST ANYTHING

Yes, you can indeed use the phone to do just about anything and, in fact, using the phone to make your organization's presence known in a reputable way in the community will benefit your fund raising efforts. For example:

- If you are a community organization planning a special event, you can call your members and invite them to participate. By getting them involved in the fun, you will get more money from them later.
- If you are a cultural organization wondering what kinds of programs to plan, you can call your members to find out what they would like. Obviously, the more they like what you plan for them, the more enthusiastic they will be and the more money they will contribute.
- If your organization is thinking of implementing a new policy, you can call your members to find out how they feel about it. After all, they are the backbone of your organization.
- If you are a political organization and crucial legislation is coming up for a vote, you can call your members to remind them that their legislators need to hear from them.
- If you are in the midst of a political campaign, you can use the phone to poll potential voters to see how they stand on the issues and on your candidate. You can also use the phone to locate volunteers and to remind people to vote on election day.
- If your organization finds itself in a tight spot, you can use the

207

phone to wiggle out. For example, organizations habitually use the phone to issue last-minute invitations or to confirm attendance when invitations were sent out late.

• Using the phone can help in times of major difficulties, also. For instance, an organization planning a well-publicized annual auction—one of its principal fund raisers—found itself with almost nothing to auction off one year. An inexperienced volunteer has been given the important job of assembling the items to be auctioned, and little had been done. Less than a week remained until the date of the auction. Squadrons of persuasive volunteers began to call individuals, local businesses, and even corporations and assembled more auctionable items in a few days than had been collected in months.

While the phone can be used to do almost anything, it should not be used in any way which will interfere with your fund raising. As you already know, it is not productive to give callers a dual mission. Do not ask a caller, for example, to be both negotiator and pollster. Polling is much easier than is telephone fund raising. If callers are asked to do both, they will excel at the former at the expense of the latter. You will end up with a wealth of information and a dearth of dollars.

The best thing to do, therefore, when you want to invite, poll, remind, request, persuade, promote, or motivate is to choose a handful of callers and let them concentrate on that task alone. The problem, then, is deciding who should work the phones to achieve these alternative goals.

Do not use your good callers. Their efforts are spent more productively on single-mindedly negotiating pledges, so do not sidetrack them.

Do not use your average callers. Inviting, polling, reminding, and the like require less assertiveness than does fund raising. If average callers use the phone to do something other than raise funds, expect them to return to fund raising less assertive, more relaxed, and way below average as callers.

How about using unproductive callers? Before firing an unproductive but reliable caller, let him try his hand at issuing invitations, polling, or whatever alternative use of the phone you need done.

The best solution, however, is not to use any of your current callers. Instead, look for new callers. These callers should be volunteers. It is easier to find volunteers to make these kinds of calls than it is to find volunteer telephone fund raisers. More people will volunteer because the task is less rigorous. Among those who volunteer, more will be suitable. You will not need to carefully weed out all those who are not superassertive. All that you really need is someone who is both articulate and polite.

You will not need to train these volunteers. Clearly, reminding people to vote, for example, does not warrant a full day of theory and practice. On the other hand, you do not want your callers to start cold. Meet with them for about an hour before they start calling. Explain to them why you need their help. Then explain what you expect them to do. To get good results, make sure your volunteers feel important. After all, they are.

Remind them to take care that neither they nor the person on the other end of the line become long-winded, a bad habit that is easy to develop when the conversation is more casual than the intense dialogue of negotiations. If it is appropriate, suggest that they ask those they call to pass on the information given them. In addition, suggest that they ask those they call for the names of friends who might support your cause, just as callers do after they negotiate a pledge successfully.

Although they will not need a formal script, you should prepare written guidelines for them. For example, a fraternal order calling to remind its members to attend the next meeting to vote in a new Board of Directors would state on its guidelines the place, date, and time of the meeting and the names of those running and their respective platforms. A church guild calling to encourage its members to work hard preparing for its annual pre-Christ bazaar would state on its guidelines how many days were left the day of the bazaar, what remained to be done, and what will be done with the money raised.

If the callers will be recording information (because they are polling, for example), make sure you have a tally sheet for them to use. Use the Refusal Tally Sheet on page 194 as a guide.

Finally, make sure callers have all the supplementary information they need. Otherwise, the call might be counterproductive. For example, not long ago an activist called a major contributor to ask him to join a vigil in front of a local hospital. The contributor, a man of status in the community, agreed to help, not by taking his place at the vigil but by calling highly placed hospital administrators, giving his name and title, and discussing the virtues of the cause with them. But the caller had no idea who those hospital administrators might be. The best the activist could do on the spur of the moment was give the contributor the hospital's phone number so he could make the inquiries himself. The man's enthusiasm waned, of course. He was willing to make a few well-placed calls, but was not willing to do groundwork that he felt the organization should have done before calling him.

INDEX